Writing

Grade 4

Printed in the U.S.A.

ISBN 978-0-5442-6848-7

4 5 6 7 8 9 10 0982 22 21 20 19 18 17 16

4500587790   B C D E F G

Core Skills Writing

GRADE 4

Table of Contents

Introduction

Writing is one of the core skills necessary for success in school and in life. The better writer a person is, the better that person can communicate with others. Good writing is a skill acquired through guidance, practice, and self-evaluation. This book provides guidance for success in different writing formats. This book also provides many opportunities for writing practice. Finally this book encourages writers to examine their own work, as well as that of their peers, and judge its qualities and flaws.

Clear writing and clear speaking are products of clear thinking. Clear thinking is a product of good organization of ideas. Good organization is a product of careful planning. One good way to plan is through graphic organizers.

- In this book, different kinds of graphic organizers are provided for students to plan their writing.

- One kind of graphic organizer, emphasized in Unit 2, allows writers to "see" their writing clearly.

- By "seeing" their writing, students can more easily determine how the different parts of a sentence work together to produce a clear expression of their main idea.

- This kind of graphic organizer allows students a more visual and tactile appreciation of their writing. It also appeals to multiple intelligences.

Organization

This book is divided into four units. Each unit builds upon earlier units. Using this scaffolded approach, students will find that writing becomes like construction. This book can help to build better writers.

- **Unit 1: Laying the Foundation** addresses basic concepts of writing, such as good writing traits and the process of writing.

- **Unit 2: Building Sentences** emphasizes the act of writing. Writers first deal with the main idea of a sentence, and then expand sentences by adding other parts of speech. By using graphic organizers, writers can visualize their sentences clearly.

- **Unit 3: Building Paragraphs** focuses on the structure and content of a well-written paragraph. Writers also learn about revising, proofreading, publishing, and self- and peer-evaluation in this unit.

- **Unit 4: Writing Forms** provides guidance and opportunities to practice writing in different formats such as narration, description, persuasion, opinion, and informative reports.

Write Away

For too many students, writing is a struggle or a pain. They may not realize the benefits of being a good writer, or they may not care. This book tries to reach out to all writers with a light tone and an approach that allows students to "see" their writing in a new light. Writing does not have to be a chore. It can be fun. Students just have to be reminded that good writing can be their golden ticket to success in school and life.

Features

The title clearly identifies the skill.

Bullets highlight important points of the skill.

Examples model the skill.

Students creatively apply the skill in **WRITE AWAY.**

The information box at the top of each page explains the skill in an interesting and lively way. Informal language encourages active participation.

A writing activity checks students' understanding.

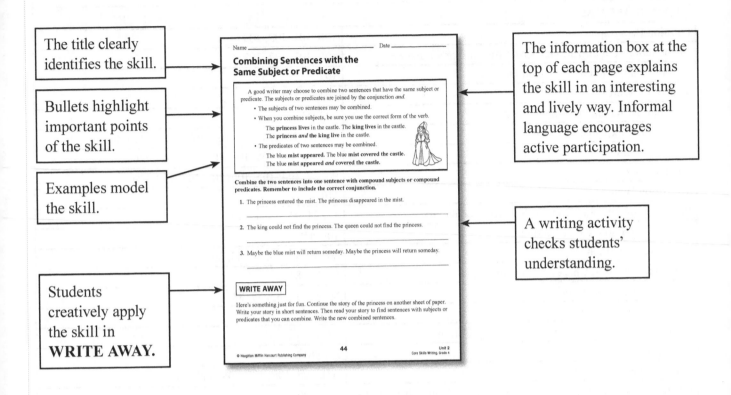

Checklists guide students through the writing process.

© Houghton Mifflin Harcourt Publishing Company

Features
Core Skills Writing, Grade 4

Skills Correlation

Skill	Page
Types of Writing	
Opinion Paragraph	100, 101, 102, 103
Introduction; Organizational Structure; Author's Purpose	100, 101, 102, 103
Reasons Supported by Facts and Details	102
Transition Words	103, 110
Concluding Statement or Section	102, 103
Informative/Explanatory Texts	95, 96, 97, 104, 105, 106, 107, 108, 109, 110
Introduction; Organization; Formatting	96, 97, 104, 105, 106, 107, 108, 109, 110
Topic Development	96, 97, 104, 105, 106, 107, 108, 109, 110
Transition Words	110
Precise Language and Domain-Specific Vocabulary	12, 24, 25, 26, 47, 105
Concluding Statement or Section	109, 110
Narrative Paragraph	80, 81, 82, 83, 84, 85, 86, 87, 88
Situation, Narrator, Characters, Event Sequence	83, 84, 85
Dialogue and Description	80, 81, 82, 85, 87, 88
Transition Words and Phrases	66, 84
Concrete Words and Phrases and Sensory Details	87, 88
Conclusion	84, 86
Short Research Project	104, 105, 106, 107, 108, 109, 110
Recall and Gather Information from Print and Digital Resources; Take Notes and Categorize Information; Provide Sources	105, 106
Draw Evidence to Support Analysis, Reflection, and Research	98, 99, 104, 105, 106, 107, 108, 109, 110
Response to Literature (Read Literary Texts)	98, 99
Read Informational Texts	97
Poem	89, 90
How-to Paragraph	93, 94
Comparing and Contrasting	71
Cause and Effect	73, 123
Summary	74, 122
Problem and Solution	72, 123
Writing Process	
Development and Organization; Task, Purpose, and Audience	2, 3, 10, 12, 13, 83, 84, 85, 86, 87, 88, 95, 96, 97, 100, 101, 102, 103, 104, 105, 106, 107, 108, 109, 110, 111
Voice	12, 68
Planning, Revising, and Editing	9, 10, 13, 15, 57, 58, 60, 67, 76, 77, 79, 107, 111, 112, 113, 114, 115, 116, 117, 118, 119
Topic	9, 11, 14, 75, 100, 101
Publishing/Publishing Using Technology	10, 78, 117, 118
Composition	
Expanding Sentences	24, 25, 26, 28, 30, 31, 32, 33, 43, 46
Paragraphs: Topic Sentence (main idea)	62, 63, 67, 69, 124
Paragraphs: Supporting Details	61, 62, 64, 69, 124

Skills Correlation, continued

Skill	Page
Composition	
Paragraphs: Concluding Sentence	61, 62, 65, 124
Time Order in Paragraphs	66
Vocabulary	
Rhyming Words	89, 90
Synonyms	49
Word Choice	12, 24, 25, 26, 47, 50, 51, 52
Sentences	
Word Order in Sentences	54, 55
Recognizing Sentences and Sentence Types	38, 39, 41
Main Idea of Sentence	17, 22
Subjects and Predicates	17, 18, 19, 20, 21, 22, 34, 35, 36, 44, 46, 51
Compound Sentences	41
Sentence Combining	43, 44, 45, 46
Sentence Fragments and Run-on Sentences	57, 58, 60
Clauses and Phrases	29, 30, 31, 32, 37
Compound Subjects and Predicates	34, 35, 36, 44
Objects	19, 22
Sentence Variety	50, 51, 54, 55, 56
Grammar and Usage	
Common and Proper Nouns	5
Singular and Plural Nouns	5
Possessive Nouns	5
Verbs and Verb Tense	6, 48
Subject/Verb Agreement	18, 36
Verb Phrases	20
Active and Passive Voice Verbs	6, 47
Pronouns	5
Articles	24
Adjectives	7, 24, 25, 28
Adverbs	7, 26, 28
Prepositions	8, 30, 31, 32, 37
Prepositional Phrases	30, 31, 32, 37
Conjunctions	8, 33, 34, 35, 36, 37, 43, 44, 45
Double Negatives	27
Capitalization and Punctuation	
Capitalization: Proper Nouns; First Word in Sentence	5, 16
End Punctuation	38, 39, 40
Commas	42, 43, 45
Quotation Marks	85, 106

Writing Rubric

Score of 4

The student:

- <u>clearly</u> follows the writing process,

- demonstrates an understanding of the purpose for writing,

- expresses creativity,

- presents the main idea and supports it with relevant detail,

- uses paragraphs to organize main ideas and supporting ideas under the umbrella of a thesis statement,

- presents content in a logical order and sequence,

- uses variety in sentence beginnings and length,

- chooses the correct writing pattern and form to communicate ideas clearly,

- clearly portrays feelings through voice and word choice,

- uses language appropriate to the writing task, such as language rich in sensory details,

- uses vocabulary to suit purpose and audience,

- summarizes main ideas when appropriate, such as in a persuasive paragraph or response to literature,

- establishes and defends a position in a persuasive paragraph, and

- has few or no errors in the standard rules of English grammar, punctuation, capitalization, and spelling.

Score of 3

The student:

- <u>generally</u> follows the criteria described above, and

- has some errors in the standard rules of English grammar, punctuation, capitalization, and spelling, but not enough to impair a reader's comprehension.

Score of 2

The student:

- <u>marginally</u> follows the criteria described above, and

- has several errors in the standard rules of English grammar, punctuation, capitalization, and spelling, which may impair a reader's comprehension.

Score of 1

The student:

- <u>fails</u> to follow the criteria described above, and

- has many errors in the standard rules of English grammar, punctuation, capitalization, and spelling that impair a reader's comprehension.

Modifiers

Adjectives and adverbs are **modifiers.** A modifier changes the meaning of another word.

dog   ➤   **green** dog

- An **adjective** modifies a noun or pronoun.

  blue sky   **funny** story   **lucky** me

- An **adverb** modifies a verb, an adjective, or another adverb.

  moved **slowly**   **very** smart   **quite** quickly

Write adjectives or adverbs to fit each writing need.

1. What adjectives could you use to write about rain?

   _____

2. What adjectives could you use to write about summer?

   _____

3. What adjectives could you use to write about where you live?

   _____

4. What adverbs could you use to write about the way you talk?

   _____

5. What adverbs could you use to write about the way people dance?

   _____

WRITE AWAY

On another sheet of paper, draw a picture. You can use a pencil, a pen, or crayons.
Then write adjectives to describe your picture.

7

Name _____ Date _____

Connectives

Conjunctions and prepositions are **connectives.** Connectives join parts of a sentence.

- A **conjunction** connects words or groups of words. Some common conjunctions are *and, or,* and *but*.

  Audrey **and** Jacob　　　here **or** there

- A **preposition** shows the relation of a noun or pronoun to another word in a sentence. Some common prepositions are *of, at, near, on, to, up, from,* and *into*.

  The purse is **under** the desk.

Draw a line between each conjunction and its meaning.

and   a choice between two things

or   a difference between two things

but   addition of two things

Write two prepositions that have a meaning similar to the given word.

4. above _____

5. below _____

WRITE AWAY

Think of prepositions that tell a location, such as *near*. Write as many as you can.

_____

_____

_____

_____

_____

8

Name _____   Date _____

The Writing Process

Have you ever sat and stared at a blank sheet of paper? Let's face it—sometimes you just can't think of anything to write. Many people have the same problem. The steps below can help you fill that blank paper with wonderful words.

1. **Prewriting**
   Prewriting is sometimes called **brainstorming.** You think about what and why you are writing. You choose a purpose and an audience. You choose a topic and make a list of your ideas. Then you organize your ideas so they make sense. The Prewriting Survey on pages 111 and 112 can help you plan your writing.

2. **Drafting**
   In the drafting step, writers put their ideas on paper. They write words, ideas, and sentences. There are often many mistakes in this step of the writing process. But that's OK! A draft is not supposed to be perfect. You just want to get all of your ideas on paper. You can fix your mistakes later.

Suppose you must clean a dirty trash can. You decide to write about it in your journal. Use the organizer to help you prewrite.

Nouns I might use: _____

Verbs I might use: _____

Adjectives I might use: _____

Adverbs I might use: _____

WRITE AWAY

Use the words above to write a few sentences about the chore.

_____

_____

_____

_____

9

The Writing Process, continued

3. Revising
In the revising step, you "see" your draft again. Read your work to be sure it makes sense. You may find new ways to arrange your ideas. You can move ideas around. You can remove or add details to make the writing clearer. You can often hear problems when you read your writing aloud. Ask someone else to read your work and give you suggestions for improvement.

4. Proofreading
When you proofread, you look at your writing carefully for mistakes. You should read your work several times to catch spelling and grammar errors. You can use the Proofreading Checklist on page 115 as a guide. A list of Proofreading Marks can be found on page 116.

5. Publishing
Publishing means "to make public." There are many ways to publish your writing. You can write it neatly or type it on a computer word-processing program. You can add pictures, a cover, and a title page. You could also share your writing by sending it in an e-mail or posting it on a class blog. Ideas for publishing using technology can be found on pages 117–118.

Write numbers 1 through 5 to show the correct order in the writing process.

_____ Begin writing. Get your ideas on paper.

_____ Check your spelling and grammar.

_____ Choose something to write about and make notes.

_____ Make a clean copy of your writing to share with others.

_____ Read your writing carefully to be sure it makes sense.

WRITE AWAY

Think about different ways you can share your writing with others. Write a sentence or two about your ideas on another sheet of paper.

Name _____ Date _____

The Seven Traits of Good Writing

When you write, you have a reason, or purpose, for writing. You might want to entertain or inform your reader. You might try to persuade your reader. There are seven **writing traits,** or skills, that will help you reach your purpose. These writing traits will help you become a better writer.

1. **Ideas**
   You write about your **ideas.** Your ideas are just as good as anyone else's. When you write, you share your ideas. So you must be sure your ideas make sense. Include enough details to make your ideas clear to the reader.

2. **Organization**
   The **organization** of your writing is the way that you group ideas and details. First, you should choose the correct form of writing for your purpose. E-mail messages, stories, reports, and journals are some writing forms. Next, your writing should have good structure. Are your ideas written in a logical order? Finally, check the first sentence. Does it grab the reader's attention? If so, the reader will keep reading. That's important!

Write a word to complete each sentence.

1. Seven writing _____ can help you become a better writer.

2. You write about your _____.

3. The way you group ideas and details in writing is your _____.

WRITE AWAY

How is a letter like an e-mail message? How are they different? Brainstorm your ideas with a friend or family member. Then write two or three sentences about your ideas on another sheet of paper.

The Seven Traits of Good Writing, continued

3. Voice

When you speak, people can tell by your voice how you feel. As a writer, you want to let the reader know what you are feeling, too. You use a writing **voice.** To share a happy feeling, you will talk about ideas that are happy. You will choose words that are happy. When you use the writing trait of voice, you make the reader feel the way you do. The voice of your writing replaces your speaking voice.

What voice would you use if someone broke your favorite CD? _____

4. Word Choice

You can choose words to make a reader feel a certain way. **Word choice** is important in other ways, too. You must be sure the reader clearly understands what you are writing about. You should choose specific words and strong action words to explain an idea.

Write a word to complete each sentence.

4. Choosing exact _____ can help you to explain an idea.

5. You use the trait of _____ to make the reader feel the way you do.

WRITE AWAY

What are some words that you could use to describe a duck? Write your words below.

_____

_____

_____

_____

_____

12

The Seven Traits of Good Writing, continued

5. **Sentence Fluency**
   Sentence fluency is when the sentences in your text flow smoothly. You want the writing to have a rhythm. When you write, read your sentences aloud. Do they flow or stumble?

6. **Conventions**
   The **conventions** are all the rules of grammar and writing. Does every sentence in your writing begin with a capital letter? Does each sentence have the correct end punctuation? Are the words spelled correctly? Follow the rules to correct the mistakes in your writing.

7. **Presentation**
   Presentation is the way your words and pictures look on the page. Your work should look neat and clean. It should be easy to read. The pictures should show the most important ideas. Don't forget to add a good title! A good title makes readers want to read your writing.

   You will use these writing traits all through the writing process. You can use the Writing Traits Checklist on pages 113–114 to help you become a better writer. Before long, your work will be better than ever!

Write a word to complete each sentence.

6. The way the words and pictures look on the page is the trait of _____.

7. The _____ are the rules of grammar and writing.

8. Sentence _____ is when the words in your sentences flow.

WRITE AWAY

How can a title make a reader want to keep on reading? What is your favorite title of all time? Why did that title make you want to read? Brainstorm your ideas with a friend or family member. Write your ideas on another sheet of paper.

13

Basic Rules of Writing

When you write, you can let your imagination run wild. You can think deeply about different topics. You can write about your most personal feelings or create fantasy lands. You never stop learning how to write. It is a fun and rewarding process. Here are a few basic rules to make you a better writer.

Pick a Topic You Are Curious About
Write about things that interest you. You will write better if you understand and feel strongly about your topic. Your reader will know that what you've written is important to you.

Stick to the Topic
Once you choose a topic, you must keep your writing focused on that topic. Decide what your reader needs to know about your topic. A good way to stick to the topic is to organize. Make an outline of what you want to write. You can write an outline on paper or create one in your mind.

Write a word to complete each sentence.

1. When you write, you can let your _____ run wild.

2. You should try to write about things that _____ you.

3. Try to keep your writing focused on your _____.

4. One way to stick to the topic is to _____.

5. A good way to organize is to write an _____.

WRITE AWAY

What are some topics that interest you? Write a list below.

_____

_____

_____

_____

Basic Rules of Writing, continued

Write Drafts

After you organize, you are ready to write the first draft. You should plan to write two or three drafts. When you write your first draft, don't worry about mistakes or neatness. The important thing is to put your ideas on paper. You can organize them better in later drafts. You can add or remove details later, too.

Reread and Edit

You don't have to be a perfect speller to be a good writer. You don't need to know all the rules of grammar, either. But you should correct as many errors as you can. Read your work over and over until you have fixed your mistakes. Try reading your work aloud. That way, both your eyes and your ears can help you catch problems. Use the Proofreading Checklist on page 115 to help you find errors. When you have corrected as many problems as you can, write your final draft.

Write a word to complete each sentence.

6. After you organize your ideas, you should write your first _____.

7. In your first draft, you want to put your _____ on paper.

8. Read your work _____ to help you catch mistakes.

WRITE AWAY

What are some other ways you can make your writing better? Write a list below.

_____

_____

_____

_____

_____

_____

15

What Is a Sentence?

> A **sentence** is a group of words that tells a complete thought. It begins with a capital letter. A sentence has two main parts, a **subject** and a **predicate.**
>
> - The <u>**subject**</u> tells who or what the sentence is about.
> - The **complete subject** is all the words in the subject.
>
>   **Big <u>lions</u>** hunt for food.
>
> - The <u>**predicate**</u> tells what the subject is or does.
> - The **complete predicate** is all the words in the predicate.
>
>   Big lions <u>**hunt**</u> **for food.**

Are the words below sentences? Write *yes* **or** *no.*

_____ **1.** Ronda runs.

_____ **2.** Jason jump

_____ **3.** Hopping horses.

_____ **4.** Tonya tumbles.

Write a word on the line to make each sentence complete.

5. _____ reads.

6. _____ writes.

7. Marta _____.

8. Erin _____.

WRITE AWAY

On another sheet of paper, write four short sentences like those above. Include a subject or a predicate and a line for the other part. Trade with a friend or family member. Complete each other's sentences.

16

The Main Idea of a Sentence

The simple subject and simple predicate form the **main idea** of the sentence.

- The **simple subject** is the main noun or pronoun in the complete subject.

- The **simple predicate** is the main verb in the complete predicate.

Ducks quack.

Ducks	quack
subject	predicate

⟵ main idea line

You can use a graphic organizer to make a diagram of the sentence. Separate the subject from the predicate with a bar. Capitalize the first word of the sentence.

Read the poem below. Complete the last two lines of the poem by writing a subject or predicate on the line. Try to make rhymes. Then write two of the sentences in the graphic organizers.

Dogs bark.

Birds fly.

_____ mew.

Babies _____.

WRITE AWAY

On another sheet of paper, write a poem like the one above. Write your poem about sounds that things make. (Horns honk.) Write each sentence in a graphic organizer that you draw.

Subject-Verb Agreement

The verb you use as a predicate in a sentence must agree in number with the subject.

- Use a **singular verb** when the subject is singular.

    A wolf howls.   ◄——— a singular verb for a singular subject

- Use a **plural verb** when the subject is plural.

    Wolves howl.   ◄——— a plural verb for a plural subject

Write a subject or verb as needed to complete each sentence. Be sure that the subject and verb agree in number.

1. Cows _____.

2. Rain _____.

3. Dogs _____.

4. A monkey _____.

5. A _____ stinks.

6. _____ sing.

7. _____ falls.

8. The _____ sets.

WRITE AWAY

This is a tough one. Some nouns can be singular or plural. One example is *sheep*. How many others can you think of? Write a list below.

_____

_____

_____

_____

Direct Objects

The main idea of your sentence may include a **direct object.** A direct object follows an action verb. It receives the action of the verb. It is part of the complete predicate. The direct object will be a noun or a pronoun.

Dogs chase cats.

Dogs	chase	cats

With a graphic organizer, you can easily see the main idea of the sentence. A long bar separates the subject from the predicate. A shorter bar separates the predicate from the direct object.

Circle the direct object in each sentence. Then write two of the sentences in the graphic organizers below. Be sure to write the subject, predicate, and object in the correct place.

1. Farmers grow corn.

2. Boys kick cans.

3. They eat watermelon.

4. Chester saw stars.

5. She called me.

6. Students write sentences.

WRITE AWAY

Add an object to complete each sentence.

I want _____.

Carlos sings _____.

Artists paint _____.

Students solve _____.

Helping Verbs

Sometimes a main verb is lazy. It needs a helper to show action and time. A **helping verb** comes before the main verb in a sentence. The main verb and its helpers form a **verb phrase.** Some common helping verbs are *am, is, are, was, were, will, must, can, may, have,* and *do.*

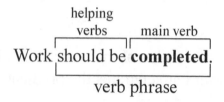

helping
verbs   main verb

Work should be **completed**.

verb phrase

The subject and verb phrase form the main idea of the sentence. The main idea may include a direct object.

He | can repair | pianos

Write a helping verb on the line to complete each sentence. Then write the first and last sentences in the graphic organizers below.

1. Birds _____ singing.

2. Eva _____ get braces.

3. I _____ hunting rocks.

4. Monkeys _____ perform tricks.

WRITE AWAY

On another sheet of paper, write five short sentences that contain helping verbs. Include direct objects in some of your sentences. Then draw five graphic organizers and write your sentences in the organizers. Be sure to write each part in the correct place.

20

Linking Verbs

What do you think a **linking verb** does? You're right. It links. A linking verb links the subject to a noun, a pronoun, or an adjective in the complete predicate. Some linking verbs are *is, are, was, were, am,* and *been.* Some linking verbs can also be action verbs. These include *feel, look, seem, smell,* and *taste.*

We are students.   I feel tired.

The linked noun or adjective is part of the main idea of the sentence. When you write a linked noun or adjective in a graphic organizer, it goes in the same place as the direct object. But the short bar leans back toward the subject. The leaning bar shows that the noun or adjective is linked to the subject.

We | are \ students   I | feel \ tired

Write a noun or adjective to complete each sentence. Then write the sentence in the graphic organizer. Be sure to write each part in the correct place.

1. Justin seems _____.

2. Emily was _____.

3. That tastes _____.

WRITE AWAY

On another sheet of paper, write five short sentences that contain linking verbs. Be sure to include a linked noun or adjective in each sentence. Then draw five graphic organizers and write your sentences in the organizers. Be sure to write each part in the correct place.

21

Review: The Main Idea of a Sentence

The main idea of a sentence is the most important part of the sentence.

- The main idea may include only a simple subject and a simple predicate. **Jacob jumped.**

- The main idea may include a simple subject, a simple predicate, and a direct object.   **Bette bought berries.**

- The main idea may include a subject, a linking verb, and a linked noun or adjective.   **We are writers.   Sara seems sick.**

Remember where each part of the sentence belongs in the graphic organizer.

| subject | verb | object |

| subject | linking verb | linked noun or adjective |

Write a sentence that will fit each graphic organizer below. Then write your sentence on the line.

1.

2.

3.

Adding Details to Sentences

The main idea tells the most important part of a sentence. But you may want to include more information. You can add **details.** Details tell more about the main idea. Details can tell whose, which, when, where, and how.

The sneaky duck stole **my jelly** sandwich.

You can see the main idea of the sentence in the graphic organizer below. All the parts of the main idea go above the main idea line. All the details go below the line. *The, sneaky, my,* and *jelly* are adjectives that modify nouns in the sentence. Place the adjectives under the words they modify.

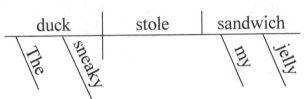

Write details on the lines to complete each sentence. Then look at the Sentence Graphic Organizers on page 120. On another sheet of paper, write each sentence in the correct graphic organizer.

1. A _____ frog croaks.

2. His dog found the _____ ball.

3. The _____ bear chased the _____ campers.

WRITE AWAY

Write details on the lines to complete each sentence. Then, on another sheet of paper, draw two graphic organizers and write your sentences in the organizers. Be sure to write each part in the correct place.

The _____ man found a _____ rock.

The _____ girl sang a _____ song.

Expanding Sentences with Adjectives

What's the difference between a red rock and a blue rock? A couple of adjectives. **Adjectives** modify nouns and pronouns. Adjectives give details that help us tell one thing from another. With adjectives, we know the difference between a sunny sky and a stormy sky.

- Look for sentences that do not express your ideas clearly.
- Think of adjectives that give a more exact picture.

The burning sun touched **the western** horizon.

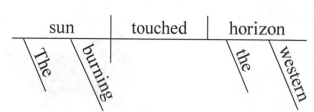

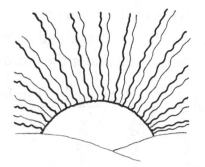

Add adjectives to expand each sentence. Write your new sentence on the line.

1. Birds sing.

   _____

2. Dogs chase cats.

   _____

3. The man carried a cane.

   _____

4. The house had cracks.

   _____

WRITE AWAY

On another sheet of paper, write adjectives that tell about each of these groups: colors, sounds, tastes, smells. See how many adjectives you can write for each group.

24

Appealing to the Reader's Senses

Writing a good description is a special skill. You can make your reader see, smell, taste, hear, or feel just as you do. To be a good descriptive writer, you must appeal to the reader's senses. Many adjectives appeal to these senses. Choose adjectives carefully. Make the reader feel that he or she is "there."

- **sight:** red, round, little, near
- **smell:** rotten, smoky, dusty
- **taste:** sour, bitter, yucky, sweet
- **hearing:** loud, quiet, squeaky
- **touch:** smooth, rough, cold

Choose adjectives that you could use to describe each object or event. Write the adjectives on the line.

1. a banana _____

2. a snowball _____

3. a fish _____

4. bread just out of the oven _____

5. the last minute in an exciting ball game _____

WRITE AWAY

Write adjectives that tell about each sense. See how many adjectives you can write for each sense.

sight _____

smell _____

taste _____

hearing _____

touch _____

Expanding Sentences with Adverbs

The difference between doing something and doing something well is an adverb. **Adverbs** describe verbs, adjectives, or other adverbs. Most adverbs tell when, where, or how. Many adverbs end in *ly*.

They will arrive **tomorrow.**   (when)
We should camp **here.**   (where)
The coyote ran **quickly.**   (how)

Adverbs are details that go under the main idea line in a graphic organizer. Write adverbs under the words they modify.

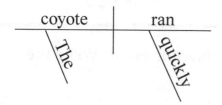

Write an adverb from the box to expand each sentence. Then look at the Sentence Graphic Organizers on page 120. On another sheet of paper, write each sentence in the correct graphic organizer.

1. The old horse walked _____.

2. Your gift arrived _____.

3. We will wait _____.

4. The boy whistled _____.

slowly
soon
yesterday
happily
here

WRITE AWAY

Write adverbs that fit each group.

tell when: _____

tell where: _____

tell how: _____

Negatives

A **negative** is a word that means "no" or "not." Many negatives are adverbs or adjectives. Some negatives are nouns or pronouns.

- *Never* and *not* are adverbs.
- *Nobody* is a pronoun.
- *No* can be a noun, an adjective, or an adverb.
- *Nothing* and *nowhere* can be adverbs or nouns.
- The negative *not* is often used in contractions.

> **Nobody** wants the rotten fruit.
> Nicki **never** eats noodles.
> He **didn't** send the letter.

Do not use two negatives, or a **double negative,** in the same sentence.

The teacher **didn't** spend **no** time on double negatives.   (incorrect)
The teacher **didn't** spend **any** time on double negatives.   (correct)
The teacher spent **no** time on double negatives.   (correct)

Choose the word in ( ) that makes the sentence complete. Write the word on the line.

1. Bailey doesn't _____ go to the library.   (never, ever)

2. He doesn't want _____ facts clogging his brain.   (no, any)

3. His parents can't do _____ with him.   (nothing, anything)

4. They can't think of _____ to help him.   (nobody, anybody)

5. Bailey says there _____ no way to make him learn.   (isn't, is)

Review: Modifiers

You can add details to a sentence by using modifiers such as adjectives and adverbs.

- An adjective modifies a noun or a pronoun.   **red** balloon
- An adverb modifies a verb, an adjective, or another adverb.

   talking **quietly**   **fairly** hot   **very** quickly

Write modifiers in the graphic organizer under the words they modify.

Write a sentence that will fit each graphic organizer below. Then write your sentence on the line.

1.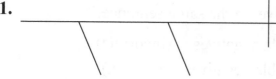

_____

_____

2.

_____

_____

3.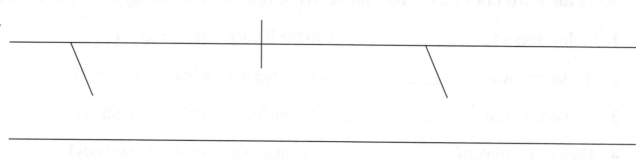

_____

_____

Clauses and Phrases

A **clause** is a group of related words that includes a subject and a predicate. An **independent clause** tells a complete thought. It may stand alone as a sentence.

Chickens cackle.

A **phrase** is a group of words that does not have a subject or a predicate. Phrases are not complete sentences. They do not tell a complete thought.

in the barnyard

You can put an independent clause and a phrase together.

Chickens cackle in the barnyard.

Circle the clause in each sentence. Draw a line under the phrase.

1. Fish swim in the pond.

2. Geese honk in the evening.

3. Jess found the puppy by the lake.

4. The girl sat on the porch.

5. In the morning, the trains run.

WRITE AWAY

On another sheet of paper, write five short clauses and five short phrases. Then cut them out. Mix and match the clauses and phrases. What funny sentences can you make?

Expanding Sentences with Prepositional Phrases

Many phrases you write will be **prepositional phrases.** A prepositional phrase is a phrase made up of a preposition, its object, and any other words.

- Remember, a preposition shows the relation of a noun or pronoun to another word in a sentence.
- Some prepositions are *of, at, in, on, to, up,* and *from.*
- The noun or pronoun that follows the preposition is called the **object of the preposition.**
- The preposition, the object of the preposition, and any other words form a prepositional phrase.

Prepositional phrases can tell where, when, whose, why, how, or which.

Astronauts fly **to the moon.** (where)
He walked **in the morning.** (when)

Add a prepositional phrase to each sentence. Your phrase should tell when, where, or both.

1. A canary lives _____. (where)

2. I found a rare coin _____. (where)

3. The stars shine _____. (when)

4. We will leave _____. (when)

5. Corn grows _____ _____. (where and when)

WRITE AWAY

On another sheet of paper, write prepositional phrases that tell where two chickens could hide in your house. (under the kitchen sink)

Expanding Sentences with Prepositional Phrases, continued

Prepositional phrases can tell where, when, whose, why, or how.

Bert found his book **under his bed.**   (where)

Bert needed his book **in the morning.**   (when)

The book also belonged **to his brother.**   (whose)

Bert needed his book **for a test.**   (why)

He found the book **with a flashlight.**   (how)

These five prepositional phrases modify the predicate. In a graphic organizer, each would be written under the predicate.

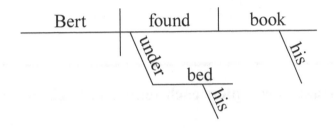

Write a prepositional phrase to complete each sentence. Look at the word in ( ) to tell what kind of prepositional phrase to write.

1. Eric went _____.   (where)

2. We did our exercises _____.   (when)

3. The muddy shoes belonged _____.   (whose)

4. Jenna read a book _____.   (why)

5. Max moved an elephant _____.   (how)

WRITE AWAY

On another sheet of paper, draw a graphic organizer for one of the sentences above. Write the sentence in the graphic organizer.

Expanding Sentences with Prepositional Phrases, continued

Prepositional phrases can also be used to tell which.

A boy **from his class** helped Bert.   (which)

The man **at the store** found my wallet.   (which)

These two prepositional phrases modify the subject. In a graphic organizer, each would be written under the subject.

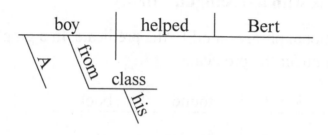

Write a prepositional phrase to complete each sentence. Each prepositional phrase should tell which.

1. A dog _____ bit him.

2. A tiger _____ roared loudly.

3. The paper _____ was ripped.

4. The boat _____ was sinking.

WRITE AWAY

Pretend you have to describe someone to the police. You have to tell which person you saw. On another sheet of paper, write as many prepositional phrases as you can think of to tell which one. (the man with purple hair)

Expanding Sentences with Conjunctions

Remember, a **conjunction** is a connective. It joins words or groups of words. Some conjunctions are *and, or,* and *but.*

Alberto **and** Rita   (*and* shows an addition)
up **or** down   (*or* shows a choice)
old **but** strong   (*but* shows a difference)

You can expand a sentence by using conjunctions. You can write compound subjects, compound predicates, compound modifiers, and compound sentences. Conjunctions are pretty handy, huh?

Write a conjunction to complete each sentence. Your conjunction should show the meaning of the word in ( ).

1. Jamil _____ Emma knew the answer.   (addition)

2. We can sink _____ swim.   (choice)

3. Slow _____ steady wins the race.   (difference)

4. Track stars run _____ jump.   (addition)

5. The food was tasty _____ tough.   (difference)

6. Kayla _____ Lex has the key.   (choice)

7. Martin is a painter _____ a poet.   (addition)

8. His uncle went to New York _____ Boston.   (choice)

WRITE AWAY

Try to count the number of times you say or write the word *and* every day. On another sheet of paper, write a few sentences about a world without conjunctions.

Compound Subjects

A **compound subject** has two or more simple subjects. The subjects are joined by a conjunction.

Carmelo *and* **Kara** danced in the contest.
Sam *or* **Sid** saw the salmon.

When you write a compound subject in a graphic organizer, you add the conjunction on a dotted line. The dotted line connects the two subjects.

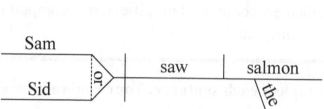

Write a compound subject to complete each sentence. Write the last sentence in the graphic organizer.

1. _____ and _____ may break my bones.

2. _____ or _____ should go to the party.

3. _____ or _____ is good exercise.

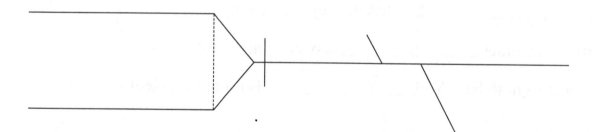

WRITE AWAY

On another sheet of paper, write five compound subjects and five predicates. Then cut them out. Mix and match the compound subjects and the predicates. What silly sentences can you make?

Name _____ Date _____

Compound Predicates

A **compound predicate** has two or more simple predicates. The predicates are joined by a conjunction.

Chickens **cluck** *and* **scratch.**
You must **pay** *or* **leave.**

When you write a compound predicate in a graphic organizer, you add the conjunction on a dotted line. The dotted line connects the two predicates.

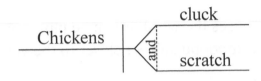

Write a compound predicate to complete each sentence. Write the last sentence in the graphic organizer.

1. Little babies _____ and _____.

2. We should _____ or _____.

3. The thunder _____ and _____.

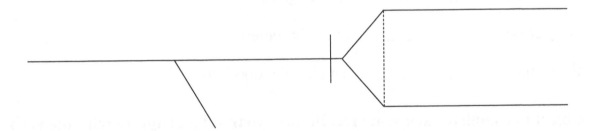

WRITE AWAY

On another sheet of paper, write five compound subjects and five compound predicates. Then cut them out. Mix and match the compound subjects and the compound predicates. Are your sentences interesting?

Agreement of Verbs and Compound Subjects

The subject of a sentence must agree in number with the verb.

- A singular subject must have a singular verb.
- A plural subject must have a plural verb.

A compound subject that uses the word *and* is a plural subject. It requires a plural verb.

Fishing *and* swimming **are** fun.

A compound subject that uses the word *or* can be plural or singular. The verb agrees with the part of the compound subject closer to the verb.

A car *or* a truck **is** a good choice.   (singular)
Carrots *or* a muffin **is** a healthy snack.   (singular)
A muffin *or* carrots **are** a healthy snack.   (plural)

Write the word *is* or *are* to complete each sentence. Be sure your verb agrees with the subject.

1. Those boys or Aron _____ guilty.

2. Checkers and chess _____ fun games.

3. Monkeys or rats _____ in the basement.

4. A wolf or snakes _____ ringing the doorbell.

Write a subject to complete each sentence. Be sure your subject agrees with the verb.

5. Funny jokes or _____ make me happy.

6. Rocks or a _____ is in the box.

7. Onions or _____ make a good sandwich.

Review: Connectives

Conjunctions and prepositions are connectives. Connectives join parts of a sentence.

- A conjunction connects words or groups of words. Some conjunctions are *and, or,* and *but.*
- A preposition shows the relation of a noun or pronoun to another word in a sentence. Some prepositions are *of, at, in, on, to, up,* and *from.*
- The preposition, its object, and any other words make up a prepositional phrase.

A graphic organizer shows the role of each connective in the sentence.

Jack **and** Jill went **up** the hill.

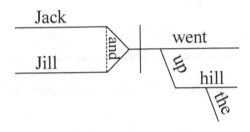

Write a sentence that will fit each graphic organizer below. Then write your sentence on the line.

1. _____

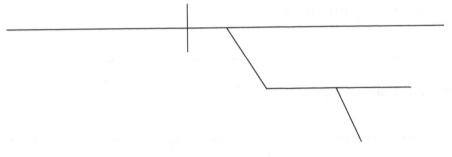

_____

2. _____

_____

37

Name _____ Date _____

Kinds of Sentences

There are four basic kinds of sentences: declarative, interrogative, imperative, and exclamatory.

- Use a **declarative sentence** to make a statement. You give information with this kind of sentence.

- Begin a declarative sentence with a capital letter. End it with a **period (.)**.

    Mosquitoes have wings.   Chickens do not have lips.

- Use an **interrogative sentence** to ask a question. You ask for information with this kind of sentence.

- Begin an interrogative sentence with a capital letter. End it with a **question mark (?)**.

    Did you see that bird?   Where are we going?

Follow the directions to write sentences. Be sure to begin and end each sentence correctly.

1. Write a declarative sentence about the moon.

   _____

2. Write an interrogative sentence about the moon.

   _____

3. Write a declarative sentence about trees.

   _____

4. Write an interrogative sentence about trees.

   _____

WRITE AWAY

On another sheet of paper, write five interrogative sentences. Then write five declarative sentences to answer your questions.

Name _____ Date _____

Kinds of Sentences, continued

There are four basic kinds of sentences: declarative, interrogative, imperative, and exclamatory.

- Use an **imperative sentence** to make a request or to give a command. You use this kind of sentence to make people do something.
- Begin an imperative sentence with a capital letter. End it with a period or an **exclamation mark (!)**.

    Please turn in your work now.   Get your stinky feet off the sofa!

- Use an **exclamatory sentence** to show excitement or strong feeling. You use this kind of sentence when you are excited.
- Begin an exclamatory sentence with a capital letter. End it with an exclamation mark.

    The tree is falling on our house!   I love exclamatory sentences!

Follow the directions to write sentences. Be sure to begin and end each sentence correctly.

1. Write an imperative sentence about doing the dishes.

   _____

2. Write an exclamatory sentence about a storm.

   _____

3. Write an imperative sentence about a box.

   _____

4. Write an exclamatory sentence about a basketball game.

   _____

WRITE AWAY

On another sheet of paper, write five imperative sentences that give a command. Then write five exclamatory sentences that respond to the commands.

End Punctuation

Be sure to use the correct punctuation at the end of your sentences.

- Use a **period (.)** at the end of a declarative sentence.
- Use a **question mark (?)** at the end of an interrogative sentence.
- Use a period or an **exclamation mark (!)** at the end of an imperative sentence.
- Use an exclamation mark at the end of an exclamatory sentence.

My pet rat is missing.   Have you seen it?

Help us look for it.   It's in the dishwasher!

Follow the directions to write sentences. Then tell what kind each sentence is.

1. Write a sentence that ends with a question mark.

   _____

2. Write a sentence that ends with a period.

   _____

3. Write a sentence that ends with an exclamation mark.

   _____

4. Write a sentence that ends with a question mark.

   _____

5. Write a sentence that ends with an exclamation mark.

   _____

6. Write a sentence that ends with a period.

   _____

A **simple sentence** is a complete sentence. It contains only one complete thought.

Bart did his homework.

But wait. You can also write a **compound sentence.**

- A compound sentence has two or more simple sentences.
- A compound sentence has two or more complete thoughts.
- A compound sentence is joined by a conjunction such as *and, or,* or *but.* You remember conjunctions, don't you?
- Use a **comma (,)** before a conjunction that joins two simple sentences.

Bart did his homework, and then his dog ate it.

Compound sentences can add variety to your writing. They change the length of some of your sentences.

Rewrite each simple sentence to make it a compound sentence. Be sure that each part of your compound sentence is a complete sentence. Remember to add a conjunction and a comma.

1. Erin ate lunch.

_____

2. Ameelya found a gold coin.

_____

3. The sky turned dark.

_____

4. Krystal heard a soft mew under the porch.

_____

5. We went to the park.

_____

41

Using Commas

Commas have many uses in sentences.

- Use a **comma** before the word *and, but,* or *or* when two sentences are joined in a compound sentence.

    The crow cawed**, and** the dark night fell.

- Use commas to separate three or more words in a **series**.

    The camper carried **a tent, a map,** and **a flashlight.**

Complete each compound sentence by adding a second sentence. Be sure to add a comma and a conjunction.

1. The crow flew away _____.

2. Thunder cracked _____.

3. Rain fell steadily _____.

Complete each sentence by adding a series of three or more words. Be sure to add commas and a conjunction.

4. The horse ran _____.

5. The goofy monkey _____.

6. _____ were in the creepy basement.

WRITE AWAY

How many series can you think of? Here's one: **the butcher, the baker,** and **the candlestick maker.** Continue the list on another sheet of paper. Remember to add commas and a conjunction.

Joining Sentences

Too many short sentences are boring. You can make your writing more interesting by joining sentences that are short and choppy.

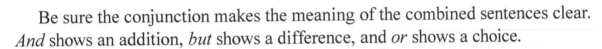

- Sentences that have ideas that go together can be joined.
- Join the sentences with a comma and a conjunction.

Be sure the conjunction makes the meaning of the combined sentences clear. *And* shows an addition, *but* shows a difference, and *or* shows a choice.

The spaceship may land on the planet. The spaceship may stay in orbit.
The spaceship may land on the planet, or it may stay in orbit.

Write a second sentence that is related to the first sentence. Then join the two sentences. Use the conjunction in ( ) to join the sentences.

1. The landing on the new planet was bumpy.   (but)

   Second sentence: _____

   Combined sentence: _____

   _____

2. Captain Karlo checked the equipment.   (and)

   Second sentence: _____

   Combined sentence: _____

   _____

3. Captain Karlo stepped out of the spaceship.   (and)

   Second sentence: _____

   Combined sentence: _____

   _____

4. The alien may greet Captain Karlo.   (or)

   Second sentence: _____

   Combined sentence: _____

   _____

Combining Sentences with the Same Subject or Predicate

A good writer may choose to combine two sentences that have the same subject or predicate. The subjects or predicates are joined by the conjunction *and*.

- The subjects of two sentences may be combined.

- When you combine subjects, be sure you use the correct form of the verb.

  The **princess lives** in the castle. The **king lives** in the castle.
  The **princess** *and* **the king live** in the castle.

- The predicates of two sentences may be combined.

  The blue **mist appeared**. The blue **mist covered the castle.**
  The blue **mist appeared** *and* **covered the castle.**

Combine the two sentences into one sentence with compound subjects or compound predicates. Remember to include the correct conjunction.

1. The princess entered the mist. The princess disappeared in the mist.

   _____

2. The king could not find the princess. The queen could not find the princess.

   _____

3. Maybe the blue mist will return someday. Maybe the princess will return someday.

   _____

WRITE AWAY

Here's something just for fun. Continue the story of the princess on another sheet of paper. Write your story in short sentences. Then read your story to find sentences with subjects or predicates that you can combine. Write the new combined sentences.

Combining Sentences to List Words in a Series

A list of three or more words or items is called a **series.** Short, choppy sentences can be combined into one longer sentence with a series.

Pet mice can be **black.** They can be **silver or white.**
Pet mice can be **black, silver, or white.**

- Look for different subjects that do the same action.
- Look for the same subject that does different actions.
- Look for different adjectives that describe the same noun.
- Look for different adverbs that modify the same word.
- Use commas and a conjunction to write a series.

    Tom is here. **Zack** is here. **Larry** is here.
    Tom, Zack, and Larry are here.

Combine each group of short sentences into one longer sentence with a series. Remember to use commas and a conjunction.

1. Jenna is studying. Carlos is studying. Ashley is studying.

   _____

2. People should eat less. People should walk more. People should exercise often.

   _____

3. Air pollution is smelly. Air pollution is dirty. Air pollution is unsafe.

   _____

4. The snow was cold. The snow was wet. The snow was mushy.

   _____

Review: Working with Sentences

You can make your writing better by using different kinds of sentences. You can make your writing livelier by joining sentences or parts of sentences.

Follow the directions to write sentences. Be sure to begin and end each sentence correctly.

1. Write a simple interrogative sentence about the circus.

   _____

2. Write a compound declarative sentence about your favorite sport.

   _____

3. Write a simple exclamatory sentence about the summer.

   _____

4. Write a compound imperative sentence about cleaning the kitchen.

   _____

5. Form a compound sentence by writing a second sentence. Be sure to add a comma and a conjunction.

   The monkey dropped from the tree. _____

   _____

6. Combine the two short sentences into one longer sentence.

   The giant snowball rolled down the hill. The giant snowball smashed into a house.

   _____

7. Combine the three short sentences into one longer sentence with a series.

   Bears ran from the snowball. Rabbits ran from the snowball. Deer ran from the snowball.

   _____

   _____

Stronger Verbs

Strong verbs make writing more lively and active. They keep your reader awake. Try this. Write a sentence and read it aloud. How does it sound? Does it make you fall asleep? Maybe you need stronger verbs. Let's test. What do you think of this sentence?

The weather **was** hot.

Pretty good, huh? Or is it? The verb *was* is rather weak. *Was* is a **passive verb.** All of the *be* verbs (*is, are, was, were, am, be, been, being*) are passive. The sentence needs an **active verb.**

The heat **crushed** us.

Crushed is an active verb. We can see the action in our heads, so we become more interested. So, to make your writing more interesting, use active verbs as much as possible.

Rewrite each sentence. Change the passive verbs to active verbs. You may have to change the way the sentence is written.

1. The smell was strong.

   _____

2. The food was salty.

   _____

3. The picture was drawn by Taylor.

   _____

4. The game was won by the Rodents.

   _____

WRITE AWAY

Here's something to do in your spare time. Make a list. Write every active verb you can think of. Use this list to help you in your future writing.

Stronger Verbs, continued

You probably remember about **verb tense.** *Tense* means "time." So verb tense tells the time the verb action is happening.

- Use a **present tense verb** to tell what is happening now.
- Use a **past tense verb** to tell what happened in the past.
- Use a **future tense verb** to tell what will happen in the future.

We **sing** now.　　　We **sang** yesterday.　　　We **will sing** tomorrow.

(present tense)　　　(past tense)　　　(future tense)

If you use the wrong verb tense, your reader will be lost in time. That's not good.

Write an active verb to complete each sentence. Use clues in the sentence to write the correct verb tense.

1. Dr. Strange _____ a robot yesterday.

2. The robot _____ now.

3. In the future, the robot _____ chores.

4. Last night, snow _____.

5. The snow _____ now.

6. Later today, it _____ again.

WRITE AWAY

Write a list of ten verbs on another sheet of paper. Then make a chart with three columns. At the top of one column, write *present tense.* At the top of the second column, write *past tense.* At the top of the third column, write *future tense.* Write your ten verbs in the correct place in the chart. Complete the chart by writing the correct tense of each verb in the columns.

Using Synonyms

> Sometimes you have to name the same thing several times in your sentences. You can use **synonyms** to make your writing more interesting. Synonyms are words that have almost the same meaning.
>
> These words are synonyms: mean   awful   hateful
>
> Do they mean the same thing? No, but they all suggest a certain way someone acts. You have to think carefully when you choose synonyms.

Write a synonym for the underlined word in each sentence.

1. Stories of the pioneers live on today.

   Synonym: _____

2. We still read stories of their journeys west.

   Synonym: _____

3. The pioneers had to be very brave.

   Synonym: _____

4. They set out across the large prairie.

   Synonym: _____

5. The pioneers faced many troubles.

   Synonym: _____

WRITE AWAY

On another sheet of paper, write a list of ten words. Then write as many synonyms as you can for each of your words.

Writing Descriptive Sentences

When you write a descriptive sentence, you want to give the reader details. Use specific details that tell who, what, when, where, and how. Your descriptive sentence should let the reader "see" the scene in his or her mind. The following tells about the object, but the reader cannot "see" the scene.

Mount Rushmore is big and wonderful.

This sentence needs more specific adjectives than "big" and "wonderful." Those adjectives only tell what you think about the object. They don't really describe the object. Here's a better descriptive sentence.

The four huge faces of Mount Rushmore stare across the dry countryside.

Good descriptive sentences use strong verbs and specific adjectives and adverbs.

Rewrite each sentence to make it more descriptive. Use strong verbs and specific adjectives or adverbs.

1. The day was cold.

   _____

2. The house was scary.

   _____

3. That woman is mean.

   _____

4. Our beach vacation was fun.

   _____

WRITE AWAY

What is your favorite possession? On another sheet of paper, write three descriptive sentences about it. Try to use strong verbs and specific adjectives or adverbs.

50

Writing Descriptive Sentences, continued

> Words are like the colors artists use to paint a picture. When you write, your words should be lively and colorful. You should include details that appeal to your reader's senses. The right words paint the perfect picture in your reader's mind. This mental picture helps your reader to understand your meaning.
>
> The **golden** sun rose over the **misty gray** mountains.
> The moon shone **dimly** through the **night** clouds.

Study each picture carefully. Then write two descriptive sentences about the picture.

1. _____

   _____

   _____

2. _____

   _____

   _____

3. _____

   _____

   _____

WRITE AWAY

Find a colorful picture or painting that you like. On another sheet of paper, write five sentences to describe it.

Using Figurative Language

Writers sometimes use **figurative language** to compare unlike things. The words in figurative language don't really mean what they say. If a man is very hungry, he might say he could eat a horse. He doesn't really mean it, though. He is using figurative language.

- A **simile** compares two things by using *like* or *as*.

  The old dog's breath smelled **like dead fish.**
  The dark night was as still **as a mouse.**

Figurative language is fun for creating mental pictures.

His truck was as big **as a house.**

Complete each simile.

1. The white clouds were like _____.

2. The autumn leaves were like _____.

3. Jacob's lunch was as big as _____.

4. The hail battered the roof like _____.

5. The rainbow was like _____.

WRITE AWAY

Rewrite each sentence below. State the same idea but use a simile.

The waves hit the beach.

_____

A dog barked in the dark night.

_____

Silly Writing

One of the best parts of writing is that you can write funny stuff. You can make up jokes. You can play with words to express silly ideas. And who doesn't like being silly sometimes?

The birds sang on the radio.
The dog's bark covered the tree.

How silly can you be? Think about each topic below. Write a silly sentence for each.

1. potatoes baked

_____

2. rain fell

_____

3. the garbage smelled

_____

4. the ocean waves

_____

WRITE AWAY

You can use silly writing to make up a joke. Write your own jokes on another sheet of paper.

What do you call a big dance for butchers?   (a meatball!)

Sentence Beginnings

Sentence variety makes your writing more interesting. Sentences that all begin the same way are boring. What about sentences that are all the same length? They are boring, too. There's an old saying that "variety is the spice of life." Well, variety is the spice of writing, too. Let's look at some ways to spice up your writing.

You can vary the beginning of a sentence.

- You can begin a sentence with an adjective.

   Angry were the voices at the meeting.

Be sure that your predicate agrees with your subject. You can use a graphic organizer to help you understand the sentence.

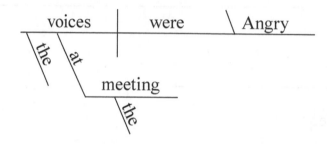

Follow the directions to write sentences. Be sure to begin and end each sentence correctly.

1. Write a sentence about clouds that begins with an adjective.

_____

2. Write a sentence about flowers that begins with an adjective.

_____

3. Write a sentence about your home that begins with an adjective.

_____

Sentence Beginnings, continued

There are many ways to vary the beginning of a sentence.

- You can begin a sentence with an adverb.
  Quickly the firefighter climbed the ladder.
- You can begin a sentence with a prepositional phrase.
  Under the house the wet cat hid.

1. Write a sentence about a brave person that begins with an adverb.

_____

2. Write a sentence about an eagle that begins with a prepositional phrase.

_____

3. Write a sentence about a river that begins with a prepositional phrase.

_____

4. Write a sentence about a duck quacking that begins with an adverb.

_____

WRITE AWAY

Write a sentence below that has at least eight words. Then think of all the different ways you could say the same thing. How many different ways can you begin the sentence? On another sheet of paper, write your sentences.

Original sentence: _____

Sentence Lengths

You can also get variety by changing the lengths of the sentences you write.

- Short sentences tell about the main idea better.

    My **friend is sick.**

- Short sentences can present actions better.

    A white **horse ran** along the beach.

- Longer sentences help to explain details better.

- Compound sentences let you tell about two related ideas.

    A **storm rolled in** across the mountains, **and Jonah quickly carried the wood** to the little cabin.

Follow the directions to write sentences. Be sure to begin and end each sentence correctly.

1. Write a short sentence that shows a main idea clearly.

    _____

2. Write a short sentence that shows a strong action.

    _____

3. Write a longer sentence with several details.

    _____

4. Write a longer compound sentence about two related ideas.

    _____

    _____

WRITE AWAY

On another sheet of paper, practice writing the same idea in sentences of different lengths. Do the shorter or longer sentences help you express yourself better?

56

Sentence Errors: Fragments

A good sentence expresses a complete idea. It has a subject and a predicate. It uses correct punctuation. But sentence errors can make your writing unclear and confusing. You need to check your writing to be sure you do not have sentence errors.

One common error is the **sentence fragment.** A sentence fragment is only a part of a sentence. It is not a complete sentence, and it does not tell a complete thought. You should remove fragments from your writing.

Had a good time at the mall.   (fragment—no subject)
Marcos and some of the other boys.   (fragment—no predicate)
At the end of the school year.   (fragment—prepositional phrases)
We learned about sentence fragments today.   (complete sentence)

Rewrite each fragment to make it a complete sentence. If the group of words is a complete sentence already, write *not a fragment*.

1. Dogs at the park.

_____

2. Two bears flew through the trees.

_____

3. Buried treasure in the backyard.

_____

4. Caught a fish at the lake.

_____

57

Sentence Errors: Run-on Sentences

Another common error is the **run-on sentence.** A run-on sentence can happen in two ways.

- A run-on happens when you join two complete sentences without any punctuation.

  We started early we still arrived late.   (run-on)

- A run-on also happens when you join two complete sentences with only a comma.

  We spent the summer in Florida, we had a good time.   (run-on)

- One way to fix a run-on is to join the two sentences with a comma and a conjunction.

  We started early, but we still arrived late.   (fixed)

- Another way to fix a run-on is to write the run-on sentence as two separate sentences.

  We spent the summer in Florida. We had a good time.   (fixed)

Correct each run-on sentence. Write the new sentence or sentences on the line.

1. He studied hard he hoped to pass the test.

   _____

2. We paddled a canoe, we swam in the lake.

   _____

3. Jana found a lost puppy it was cold and wet.

   _____

4. Kyle searched for the keys, he could not find them.

   _____

Seeing Your Writing

If you can see—not read, but see—your writing, you have a better idea of each part's role in the sentence. You can see the main idea of the sentence and the location of details. Seeing your writing can help you organize better.

Match each sentence on the left to its graphic organizer on the right. Write the letter of the organizer before the sentence. You may write on the graphic organizers.

_____ 1. Wolves howl.　　A.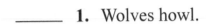

_____ 2. Hashi held a hamster.　　B.

_____ 3. Grandpa called yesterday.　　C.

_____ 4. The check is in the mail.　　D.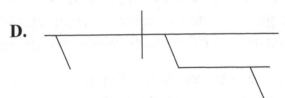

_____ 5. The black hat on the chair is mine.　　E.

Self-Evaluation: What's Going On?

You've been studying hard, of course, and writing all these sentences. Did you learn anything? Do you think you are a better writer now? Do you know what a good sentence is? Well, on this page you will get a chance to show your stuff.

Each of the following sentences has one or more errors. Study each sentence. Then rewrite each sentence correctly.

1. Did you see those flying saucers.

_____

2. I didn't see no flying saucers?

_____

3. The three dogs eats a apple.

_____

4. I found money at the mall, I gave it to the guard.

_____

WRITE AWAY

You should take your time on this part. You want to do your best writing. First, on another sheet of paper, write two sentences that tell about something you really like. Pretend the sentences are your first draft. Write quickly and get your ideas on paper.

Next, revise your sentences. Do the sentences say what you mean? Will your reader understand your meaning? Can the word choice be improved? Think about your sentences for five minutes. Read them aloud once or twice. Then write each sentence three different ways. Read each sentence aloud as you are writing it. How does it sound?

OK, now choose the best one of each sentence. Write the two sentences in final form. Compare your sentences to the Self-Evaluation Checklist on page 119. Check each point that agrees with your writing. How good is your writing? On another sheet of paper, write three or four sentences that describe your writing style.

What Is a Paragraph?

A **paragraph** is a group of sentences that tells about one main idea. A paragraph has three parts.

- The **topic sentence** tells the main idea of the paragraph.
- The **detail sentences** tell more about the main idea.
- The **concluding sentence** closes the paragraph. It restates the main idea and summarizes the information in the paragraph.

Read each paragraph below. How well does each paragraph tell about one main idea? Write a few sentences about each paragraph. Tell why it is or is not a good paragraph.

The rattlesnake is a poisonous snake in the United States. Its fangs and well-known rattle scare many people. Bears are pretty scary, too, and so are rats. Rats are probably the worst. They creep around while you are sleeping. At least rattlesnakes don't have hair. The rattlesnake can be dangerous, so watch out!

_____

_____

_____

_____

Many people like to track the phases of the moon. The moon goes through a monthly cycle. It has eight phases, from a new moon to a full moon and back to a new moon. The phase may be a waxing crescent or waning gibbous. It may be in the first quarter or the last quarter. Look at the moon tonight and have fun guessing the phase.

_____

_____

_____

_____

What Is in a Paragraph?

A paragraph is a group of sentences about one main idea. The first sentence of the paragraph is **indented.** There are usually several sentences in a paragraph. Many paragraphs have five sentences.

- The **topic sentence** names the topic or main idea of the paragraph.
- The **detail sentences** give specific information about the topic.
- The **concluding sentence** restates the main idea and sums up the information in the paragraph.

Read the paragraph below. Then write sentences to answer each question.

Eating spaghetti is fun, but it can be a little dangerous. The fun part of eating spaghetti is the sound and taste. The slurping sound is a little rude, but it reminds me how much I love spaghetti. The dangerous part is when the food on your fork falls off. The meatball can fall in your lap, and the spaghetti sauce can get all over your clothes. For me, spaghetti is the perfect meal, even if it is messy.

1. What is the topic of this paragraph?

   _____

2. Write the topic sentence from the paragraph.

   _____

   _____

3. Write a detail sentence from the paragraph.

   _____

   _____

4. Write the concluding sentence from the paragraph.

   _____

   _____

Writing a Topic Sentence

A **topic sentence** tells the topic or main idea of a paragraph. The topic sentence is usually the first sentence in a paragraph. A topic sentence should have **focus.** Focus means you have narrowed down the topic. For example, you might have the general topic of dogs. You could focus on dogs used to herd cows.

Kacy decided she needed a new hobby. She thought about different things she could do. She thought about collecting toothpicks or paper clips. Maybe she could start making quilts. Kacy finally decided to write a family history as her new hobby.

Read each topic below. Then choose a focus for each topic. Write a topic sentence that you could use to write a paragraph about your topic.

1. Topic: mountains

   Focus: _tallest mountains_

   Topic sentence: _The tallest mountain in the United States is Mount McKinley._

2. Topic: oceans

   Focus: _____

   Topic sentence: _____

3. Topic: pets

   Focus: _____

   Topic sentence: _____

WRITE AWAY

On another sheet of paper, write a paragraph using one of your topic sentences.

Writing Detail Sentences

The body sentences in a paragraph are **detail sentences.** Detail sentences give facts or examples about the topic. Detail sentences help the reader learn more about the topic.

You need to choose your details carefully. A good plan is to list all the details you can think of. Then choose the three details that best support the topic sentence. Include the details in three body sentences.

Kacy decided she needed a new hobby. **She thought about different things she could do. She thought about collecting toothpicks or paper clips. Maybe she could start making quilts.** Kacy finally decided to write a family history as her new hobby.

Complete the prewriting steps below. What does winter make you think of? Write some details. Then narrow your thoughts on winter to the given topic sentence.

Topic: winter

Details about winter: _____

_____

_____

Topic sentence (focus): Winter weather often causes problems for people.

Choose three best details from above for this topic sentence:

_____

_____

_____

Write three detail sentences that support the topic sentence.

_____

_____

_____

Writing a Concluding Sentence

A **concluding sentence** ends the paragraph. It restates the topic sentence in different words. It sums up the information in the paragraph.

Pretend that your paragraph is a sandwich. The two slices of bread hold all the details inside—the peanut butter, the jelly, the pickle slices. The top slice of bread is like the topic sentence. The bottom slice of bread is like the concluding sentence. Read the paragraph about Kacy and her new hobby. The concluding sentence is like the topic sentence but not exactly.

Kacy decided she needed a new hobby. She thought about different things she could do. She thought about collecting toothpicks or paper clips. Maybe she could start making quilts. **Kacy finally decided to write a family history as her new hobby.**

Read the paragraph below. Then write two possible concluding sentences for the paragraph. One possible concluding sentence is done for you.

Over the years, people have thought of many ways to cure the common cold. People today usually take a pill to treat their cold. Years ago, some people believed a dead frog could cure a cold. The sick person had to wear the dead frog on a necklace for two weeks.

Concluding sentence 1: _Some of the cures were strange and probably_

didn't work. _____

Concluding sentence 2: _____

_____

Concluding sentence 3: _____

_____

Name _____ Date _____

Using Time Order in Paragraphs

A paragraph should have a beginning, a middle, and an end. You can join the parts of the paragraph by using **transition** words. **Time-order words** are one kind of transition. Some words that show time order are *before, after, first, next, then,* and *finally*. Read the sample paragraph. Notice how the time-order words help you read smoothly through the paragraph.

The weather began to turn stormy. **First**, the wind began to blow. **Next**, the sky turned dark. **Then**, lightning flashed and thunder rumbled. **Finally**, sheets of rain started to fall. A big thunderstorm had arrived.

Number the sentences in the order the events happened. The topic sentence is numbered for you. Then write the sentences in paragraph form on another sheet of paper. Remember to indent the first sentence.

__1__ May 18, 1980, was strangely quiet until Mount St. Helens shook.

_____ Finally, the north side of the mountain blew off.

_____ Then, long cracks opened in the ground.

_____ Next, hot gases trapped inside the mountain exploded out through the cracks.

_____ First, the slopes of the mountain crumbled and slid into the valley below.

_____ Mount St. Helens had erupted!

Prewriting a Paragraph

If only words would appear magically from your pen! Of course, they don't. So you have to think about what you will write. In **prewriting,** you think about what you will write. Prewriting is sometimes called **brainstorming.** Prewriting has three main steps.

- think
- choose
- organize

Prewriting is an important skill to practice. When you prewrite, you work on ideas and words in your mind more than on paper. The Prewriting Survey on pages 111–112 can help you with prewriting. You can also use the Paragraph Structure Chart on page 124 to help you build your paragraph.

You have an assignment to write a paragraph on your personal feelings about your home. Do some prewriting. Think about what you must write. Fill in the chart below to help you prewrite.

Main goal of assignment: _____

Nouns I might use: _____

Verbs I might use: _____

Adjectives I might use: _____

Adverbs I might use: _____

WRITE AWAY

Pretend that you have been elected president. Write a few words you might use in your acceptance speech.

_____

_____

Voice

When you talk to others, they can tell how you feel by listening to your voice. In writing, **voice** is the way a writer "speaks" to the readers. Voice is how your writing sounds. The readers can "hear" how you feel about the topic. Your voice should fit your topic.

- Don't write cheerfully about people crying as they wave good-bye to friends.
- Do write cheerfully about people celebrating a holiday.

To choose your voice for a topic, you must think of your audience. Who will read your writing? Your voice should also fit your audience.

Write a sentence to describe the voice in each paragraph. Is the voice serious, funny, happy, sad, or some other emotion?

1. I sat quietly and watched the last leaf fall from the old oak tree. I shivered as I thought of the coming winter.

    _____

2. Pollution is a problem in today's world. Our air and water are getting more polluted. We must do something about pollution before it's too late.

    _____

3. Rex was hungry, and he was going to do something about it. First, he got out the bread. Then, he found a jar of peanut butter. He took the jelly bottle from the refrigerator and almost dropped it. His sandwich was almost ready when his owner entered the kitchen. She had never seen a dog make a sandwich before.

    _____

WRITE AWAY

On another sheet of paper, write a short paragraph about your pet lizard that has run away. Use a sad voice.

Writing Pattern: Main Idea and Details

Writing patterns can help you organize your work. Choosing a pattern in the prewriting step will help you choose a writing form. For example, suppose you wanted to tell your friend how to clean your hamster's cage while you were on vacation. You would write the steps in order. You would use the sequence of events pattern to tell what to do first, next, and last.

You already know about main idea and details. The main idea is the most important idea. The details tell more about the main idea. Details give a clearer picture of the main idea. You might choose to describe something using your senses. When you choose this pattern, the Main Idea and Details Web on page 121 can help you plan your work.

Think about a glass of milk. Suppose you have to describe it in an assignment. Use the Main Idea and Details Web on page 121 to write details about the drink. Follow the directions to complete the organizer.

1. What is the topic or main idea? Write it in the center oval.

2. Which senses can you use to describe the drink? How does it look? What color is it? How does it smell? How does it feel if you touch it? How does it taste? Write one detail in each circle. Draw more circles around the center oval if necessary.

3. What are some words that describe each detail? Write specific adjectives, adverbs, and nouns that you could use to write a paragraph.

On another sheet of paper, write a paragraph that describes the glass of milk. Use your organizer to help you write.

Writing Pattern: Sequence of Events

Sometimes you must write about an event or tell how to do something. Be sure to tell the action or steps in order. What if you were baking a pie? You would have a mess if the directions didn't tell you to put the pie crust in the baking dish first.

Narratives and how-to directions use events in order. In both kinds of writing, you would choose a writing pattern that shows the **sequence,** or order, of events. When you choose this pattern, a sequence chart can help you plan your work. It helps you think about each step. You can plan which time-order words to use. Some time-order words are *first, next, then,* and *finally.* You can make your own chart like the one below. Add as many boxes and time-order words as you need.

First,	Next,	Finally,

Tell how to make a peanut butter and jelly sandwich. On another sheet of paper, draw a sequence chart to write the steps in order. Follow the directions below to complete the chart.

1. Which step do you do first? Write it in the first box.

2. Which step do you do last? Write it in the last box.

3. Which steps do you do in between? Write time-order words in the boxes. Then write the steps. Draw more boxes if necessary.

WRITE AWAY

On another sheet of paper, write a paragraph that tells how to make a peanut butter and jelly sandwich. Follow the steps in your organizer.

Writing Pattern: Compare and Contrast

When you **compare** and **contrast,** you tell how two things are alike and different. If you compare your bedroom to the kitchen, you could say that both rooms have walls, doors, and windows. To contrast them, you could say that your bedroom is for sleeping and the kitchen is for cooking. They have different furniture in them. The two rooms are alike and different at the same time.

This writing pattern is useful if you want to inform your reader how two things are similar or different. When you choose this pattern, a Venn diagram can help you plan your work. It helps you think about how the two items are related.

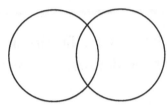

Compare and contrast a fork and a spoon. Draw a bigger Venn diagram like the one above. Follow the directions below to complete the diagram.

1. Label each circle with a utensil name. Write *fork* above one circle. Write *spoon* above the other circle.

2. Look where the circles overlap. Write words that tell how the utensils are alike in this space. For example, you might write *used for eating* or *made of metal.*

3. In the circle under *fork*, write words that describe the fork. The words should tell how it is different from the spoon. Think about its shape, size, and use.

4. In the circle under *spoon,* write words that describe the spoon. The words should tell how it is different from the fork. Think about its shape, size, and use.

WRITE AWAY

On another sheet of paper, write a paragraph that compares and contrasts a fork and a spoon. Use the details in your Venn diagram.

Writing Pattern: Problem and Solution

A **problem** is something that is wrong. It needs to be fixed. A **solution** is the way to fix the problem. The problem and solution writing pattern is useful to get the audience to agree with your solution. It can also be used to explain something that is a problem.

When you use this pattern, be sure that the audience understands the problem. Give examples and details that are clear and specific. Explain why the solution works. When you choose this pattern, the Problem and Solution Chart on page 123 can help you plan your work.

Think about a problem that you had with a family member. Use the Problem and Solution Chart on page 123 to list the details. Follow the directions below to complete the chart.

1. Write the problem. Give an example and list two or three details about the problem.

2. Write the solution. Be specific. Tell why the solution would work.

WRITE AWAY

On another sheet of paper, write a paragraph that tells about the problem that you had with a family member. Explain the solution. Use the details in your organizer.

Writing Pattern: Cause and Effect

A **cause** is <u>why</u> something happens. An **effect** is <u>what</u> happens. For example, suppose you are eating ice cream on a hot day. The ice cream melts faster than you can eat it. In this example, the cause is the heat. The effect is that the ice cream melts.

The example above is a simple cause and effect event. However, one cause and effect pair can lead to a chain of cause and effect pairs. Think about the ice cream example above. Suppose some of the melting ice cream drips on your toe. A bug comes to eat the ice cream that dripped. The bug bites your toe, which causes you to hop up and spill all the ice cream. As you can see, each effect can lead to another cause. Each cause can lead to another effect.

This writing pattern is useful if you are telling about why events happen. You should clearly state the cause and the effect so that a reader can understand the why and what of an event. You can use the Cause and Effect Chart on page 123 to help you plan your work.

Think about a time you had an accident. Use the Cause and Effect Chart on page 123 to explain the details. Follow the directions below to complete the chart.

1. Write the cause. Use specific nouns and verbs to explain the details.

2. Write the effect, or what happened. Use sense words so that the audience can "see" the effect.

WRITE AWAY

On another sheet of paper, write a paragraph that tells about a time you had an accident. Clearly explain the cause and the effect.

Writing Pattern: Summarize

Think about the last book you read. If someone asked you about it, what would you say? Would you describe what you wore while you were reading? Would you tell where you sat while you read? Probably not. Instead, you would tell the most important details about the book. You would also tell what happens in the book.

When you **summarize,** you tell the most important details about something. You tell who, what, where, when, why, and how. You might use this writing pattern if you wanted to give your audience a short description of a book or story. Remember, give the most important details so the audience understands the topic, but be brief. You can use the Summary Chart on page 122 to help you plan your work.

Think again about the last book you read. Use the Summary Chart on page 122 to list the most important details. Follow the directions below to complete the chart.

1. Write the important details about the book on the left side of the box. Tell who, what, where, when, why, and how. You do not need to write complete sentences.

2. Use the details from the left side of the chart to tell about the book. Do not include any extra information. Write as few sentences as you can, but be sure to include all the important details. Be sure to name the book you are summarizing.

WRITE AWAY

On another sheet of paper, write a paragraph that summarizes the book you read. Name the book in your summary. Don't forget to include a topic sentence and a concluding sentence!

Keeping to the Topic

A paragraph should have **unity.** That means all the parts work together to tell about one main idea. One way to get unity is to stay on topic. Be sure your paragraph doesn't have **unnecessary information.**

Pretend that you and four friends are sitting at a table somewhere. You're working on a project, and everyone is happy to be together. Everyone joins in the conversation. The group is like a good paragraph. Then a stranger sits down at your table. The stranger doesn't know anything about the project. She doesn't really fit with your group. The stranger is like unnecessary information in a paragraph. It doesn't belong with the other information. When you write a paragraph, keep to the topic and remove details that do not support the main idea.

Read each paragraph carefully. Mark out the unnecessary information in the paragraph. Then write why the information is not needed.

1. The dingo is a wild dog. It lives in Australia. Kangaroos live in Australia, too. Dingoes usually howl instead of barking. They can make good pets if they are caught as puppies.

   _____

   _____

2. To write a family history, Kacy would have to talk to many family members. She would have to ask many questions. Kacy thought about the kinds of questions she would ask. She went to the store and bought some pickles for her sandwich. She wrote a list of questions she would ask each family member. Then Kacy was ready to talk to members of her family.

   _____

   _____

Revising

You must write in a way that other people can understand your meaning. Maybe you can read what you have written and know what it means, but will your reader be able to? That's where revising comes in. *Revising* means "seeing again."

To revise, pretend that you are reading someone else's writing. Then read what you have written. Read it aloud. You want the writing to seem new and fresh to you. Ask yourself some questions about what you have read.

- Is the writing clear and direct?
- Are the sentences complete ideas?
- Are the verbs active?
- Are the adjectives and adverbs clear and specific?
- Does the paragraph make sense?

The last question is probably the most important one. If you can't understand what you wrote, then your reader won't understand either. You have to revise the writing until it makes sense.

Read the following paragraph. It is not very well written. Revise the paragraph on another sheet of paper. To revise, you must do more than correct grammar errors. You can add details and change sentences. You must improve the writing and make it clearer for the reader.

We went to this place for our summer vacation. It was somewhere. There were these little cabins that people stayed in, and we stayed in one. There was some water nearby. It was a lake. There were lots of mosquitos, and they bit me.

Name _____   Date _____

Proofreading a Paragraph

> Revising deals with improving the content of your paragraph. **Proofreading** deals with correcting your writing. When you proofread, you look for errors you have made. When you **edit,** you correct those errors. To be a good proofreader, look for one kind of error at a time.
>
> - capitalization
> - punctuation
> - spelling
> - grammar
>
> An error-free paragraph is much easier to read. Complete the Proofreading Checklist on page 115. Use the chart of Proofreading Marks on page 116 to help you edit your writing.

Proofread the following paragraph. Pay attention to the kinds of errors listed above. Use the Proofreading Marks on page 116 to mark the errors. You should find at least ten errors.

Windmills are macheens that use wind power. they are used to

provide powwer to pump water or to generate electricity. Most

windmills has a wheel of blades that is turned by the wind. The

shaft of the wheel are mounted on a tower the shaft is connected

to a system of gears. These geers carry power to a watter pump or

an electric generator

WRITE AWAY

On another sheet of paper, write why you think proofreading and editing are important steps in writing.

Publishing

Once you have revised and edited your writing, you are ready to **publish** it. *Publish* means "to make public." In other words, you share your writing with others.

There are many ways to share your writing. You can make a paper copy with a title page and pictures. You can send your writing in an e-mail. You can post it to a class blog.

When you finish editing, write your final draft. Your final draft should be neatly written or typed. It should be free of errors. It should be the best you can write.

Ask your teacher how you will share your writing. If you are making a paper copy, follow these steps.

- Make a title page for your work.
- Think of a great title. Focus on words that are in your writing.
- Add pictures that might help to explain your writing.
- Use charts or bullets if needed to help your reader understand.

Instead, you might use technology to publish your writing. Pages 117–118 tell you how to write an e-mail and a blog entry.

If you have done your best, the publishing part should be the most fun step in the writing process.

Pretend that you have just finished a report about tornadoes. Make a title page for your report. Include a title and a picture.

Self-Evaluation: What's Going On?

In writing, there are two kinds of eyes—the writer's eyes and the reader's eyes. When you write, you use the writer's eyes. You see the words you have written through the writer's eyes. When you read someone else's writing, you use the reader's eyes.

A good writer has both kinds of eyes. The writer uses the writer's eyes while writing. Then, to revise, the writer uses the reader's eyes.

A good writer can tell how good his or her writing is. Self-evaluation can help you tell how good a writer you are.

Write a paragraph below. Use another sheet of paper if necessary. You can write about your favorite memory or a topic of your choice. Be sure to include a topic sentence, detail sentences, and a concluding sentence. Do your best writing.

Get a copy of the Self-Evaluation Checklist on page 119. Compare your paragraph to the checklist points. Check each point that agrees with your opinion of your writing. How good is your writing? What are the strengths and weaknesses of your writing? What can you do to improve your writing? On another sheet of paper, write a paragraph that describes your writing style. Then write a paragraph that tells how you can improve your writing.

_____

_____

_____

_____

_____

_____

_____

_____

Writing a Descriptive Paragraph: Person

When you **describe,** you paint a picture using words. You want the reader to "see" the thing you are describing. In fact, a good description lets the reader see, feel, hear, taste, and smell the thing. When you describe, you want to appeal to the reader's senses. The reader should feel as if he or she is with you examining the thing. Remember to use your writing voice when you describe. You can describe people, places, or things.

When you describe a person, give unique details about the person. Most people have two ears, a nose, two arms, and so on. So you don't really have to deal with common details. First, give an overall view. Then give specific details.

Uncle Mike was a big man. But his arms seemed too thin and his hands too small for a man his size. On his left hand, half of one of his fingers had been cut off. He enjoyed telling stories about how he had lost that finger. The stories often included alligators or bears. As he told the stories, he would rub his pointed chin with his rough hands. His deep voice made him seem scary and friendly at the same time.

First, choose a person to describe. Next, write a list of details you will use to describe that person. Remember to use unique details that appeal to the reader's senses. Then, on another sheet of paper, write a paragraph describing that person.

Person I will describe: _____

Descriptive details I will use: _____

_____

_____

_____

_____

Writing a Descriptive Paragraph: Place

When you write a descriptive paragraph, write a topic sentence that tells what you are describing. Add detail sentences that give specific information about your topic. Use lively and colorful words to describe the topic. Paint a clear picture for your reader with the words you choose.

When you describe a place, give details that make the reader feel as if he or she is there.

- Group details in a way that makes sense.
- Lead the reader through the place. Use movements such as front to back, top to bottom, or outside to inside.
- Be sure your topic sentence names the place you are describing.

The old house was half hidden by overgrown weeds. Shingles flapped on the roof, and the chimney was crumbling. Broken windows on each side of the front door told the sad story. No one had lived there for a long time. The front door creaked as it swung open. Inside the house, the air was cold and damp. Thick dust covered everything. The old house seemed to hold many memories.

Think of a place to describe. Then complete the graphic organizer below. Write the place in the circle. Write descriptive details on the lines. Use the graphic organizer to write a descriptive paragraph on another sheet of paper. Be sure to use movements that lead your reader around.

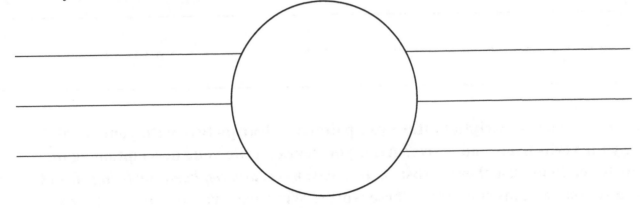

Core Skills Writing, Grade 4

Writing a Descriptive Paragraph: Thing

Remember that a description paints a picture in words. You want your reader to see, hear, feel, smell, and taste what you are describing. Use colorful and specific adjectives as you describe. Use lively and active verbs, too.

When you describe a thing, identify it in your topic sentence.

- Use sensory words as you describe.
- Pretend that your reader is looking over your shoulder.
- Will your reader experience the thing as you do?

The golden ring shines brightly in the warm sunlight. The cool metal ring fits snugly on my finger. The green stone on the ring glows like a green star. I can see my reflection in the golden metal. That tells me the wonderful ring belongs to me.

Think of a thing to describe. It should be small, such as something you can hold in your hand. Then write a rough draft of your description. Name your thing in the topic sentence. Be sure to include sensory words.

_____

_____

_____

_____

_____

_____

_____

Now revise your description. Have you painted a clear picture with your words? Are your verbs lively and active? After you revise, write your description again. This time, do not use these verbs: *is, are, was, were, am, be, been,* or *being*. Don't use any contractions containing these words. Write your revision on another sheet of paper.

Writing a Narrative Paragraph

When you **narrate,** you tell about a **sequence** of events. Often the sequence tells what happens in a story. A story is also known as a **narrative.** The narrative can be fact or fiction. A narrative should have a beginning, a middle, and an ending. To write a narrative paragraph, follow these steps.

- Write an interesting beginning. Present your main **character** and the **setting.** (The beginning is like a topic sentence.)
- Tell about a problem the main character has to solve in the **middle.** Tell what happens in order. (These are the detail sentences.)
- Write an **ending.** Tell how the main character solves the problem. This is also called the **outcome.** (The ending is like a concluding sentence.)
- Give your narrative a title.

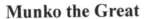

Munko the Great

Munko was a clumsy magician. He often dropped his wand. Sometimes he would sneeze and make a rabbit disappear. But he always got the rabbit back, sooner or later. One night Munko sneezed while doing a big trick. Suddenly Munko vanished. No one has seen him since then. Munko really was a clumsy magician.

Write a short silly narrative like the story of Munko. First, introduce the narrative with a general statement. Then, give specific details to tell what happens in the narrative. When the events have ended, give a general statement about the outcome. Use another sheet of paper.

Personal Narrative

A **personal narrative** is a story about something you have done. Include your feelings and your writing voice in your personal narrative. The purpose of a personal narrative is to tell about you.

- Write from your point of view. Use words such as *I, me,* and *my* to tell your story.
- Think about the details of the story. What do you want to tell the reader?
- Organize the events into beginning, middle, and ending.
- Write an interesting beginning that "grabs" your readers.
- Give details that help the reader understand what is happening.
- Write the ending from your point of view.
- Remember to use your writing voice to tell the story.

My Night of Fright

I remember the night I spent in the haunted house. My friends had dared me to do it. I thought I wouldn't be scared. Boy, was I wrong! The old house groaned and creaked all night long. Strange noises filled every closet. Around midnight a big rat ran across the floor! I did not sleep at all that night. There was no way I would close my eyes. Finally the beautiful sun came up the next morning. My night of fright was over. I promised myself I would never do such a silly thing again.

> The word *Finally* is a transition word. It helps the reader understand the order of events. Use transitions like *second, after, next, then, because,* and *later* to show the order events happened.

Write a personal narrative paragraph about something scary that has happened to you. Be sure to have a beginning, a middle, and an ending in your narrative. Remember to indent the first line of your paragraph. Use another sheet of paper.

Characters and Dialogue

A narrative usually includes characters. **Characters** are real or made-up people or animals. They act in the events. Before you write, you must decide who your characters will be. In a personal narrative, the characters will probably be you and your friends, family members, or pets. If you make up characters, decide what kind of characters they will be. How will they act? What will they do?

Characters usually speak in narratives. What they say is called **dialogue.** If you write dialogue, you must follow some rules.

- Place **quotation marks (" ")** before and after the speaker's exact words.
- Use a comma to separate dialogue from the rest of the sentence unless a question mark or exclamation mark is needed.
- Begin a new paragraph each time the speaker changes.
- Be sure the dialogue sounds like real people talking.

After the Night of Fright

"So, how was the haunted house?" Levon asked me the next day.

"It was fun," I lied. "Why don't you do it?"

"Because I'm not that brainless," Levon said, acting tough. He turned and rode his bike up the street. I bet he was just scared.

Write some lines of dialogue to include in your personal narrative about a scary event. Begin a new paragraph each time the speaker changes. Remember to put quotation marks before and after the dialogue. Then rewrite your personal narrative on another sheet of paper. Add dialogue to make your narrative more interesting.

Setting

A narrative must have a setting. A **setting** is where and when the events take place. Like characters, settings can be real or fictional. A good setting makes a narrative more interesting and exciting. Use details in your setting to make your characters and the problem seem more realistic.

A Scary Sight

We watched the strange figure stumble across the dark field. We could hear its heavy breathing. Suddenly the clouds parted, and the moon shone through. We saw an ugly face in the moonlight. It was coming right toward us!

Make up an idea for a narrative. Then complete the story chart below. Identify the main character and other characters. Tell the problem. List some events that happen as the main character tries to solve the problem. In the ending, tell what finally happens. What is the outcome? How is the problem solved? Describe the setting. You will write your narrative soon!

Beginning	Middle	Ending
Characters: Setting:	Problem:	Outcome:

Using Concrete Words and Phrases

When you tell a story, what helps your reader know exactly what you mean? One thing that helps is to use **concrete**, or specific, **words and phrases.** Notice the difference between these pairs of descriptions. The first sentences don't tell you very much! The second sentences give you more details.

General words and phrases:	→	**Concrete words and phrases:**
The person had something to drink.	→	The police officer drank a cold soda.
The vehicle went to the accident.	→	The ambulance sped toward the five-car pileup.
The child made a face.	→	The four-year-old boy poked out his tongue.

Read these sentences. Look at the underlined words. Rewrite each sentence and use a concrete, or specific, word or phrase to replace each underlined word. See how specific you can be!

1. The person bought something at the store.

   _____

2. The room was filled with stuff.

   _____

3. The children saw animals at the zoo.

   _____

4. The adult handed the person something.

   _____

WRITE AWAY

Think about concrete words you can use in your narrative. On your own paper, write a list.

Using Sensory Details in a Narrative

Sensory details are words that appeal to the five senses: sight, smell, taste, hearing, and touch. (You can read page 25 for more information about appealing to the five senses.)

Read the narrative below. Notice how the author appeals to different senses.

Painting the Sky

One morning, the fourth-graders couldn't believe their eyes! Their classroom was filled with 25 red balloons with long strings.

"Grab a balloon," said Mrs. Gupta. "We're going outside."

The children grabbed a balloon. They marched outside behind Mrs. Gupta. They smelled freshly cut grass and felt a cool breeze on their skin.

"OK," said Mrs. Gupta. "It's time to paint the sky."

"Paint the sky?" cried the children. They giggled.

"Yes," said Mrs. Gupta. "Pretend your balloons are paintbrushes. The sky is your paper. What will you paint?"

The children stood very still. No one made a sound. Then, little Henry started to run.

"Choo! Choo! I'm painting a train!" he said as he made the shape of a train with his balloon. The other children laughed as Henry ran in circles to "paint" wheels. They spent the rest of the afternoon painting the clear blue sky.

Write the sensory details that describe a sight, a smell, a feeling, and a sound from "Painting the Sky."

_____

_____

WRITE AWAY

Look at your story chart on page 86. Write your narrative on another sheet of paper. Include dialogue, concrete words and phrases, and sensory details.

Writing a Poem

Poems are fun to write. You can play with words and tell your feelings. You can rhyme words and paint a word picture.

- **Rhyming words** have the same sounds.

    new—blue   sky—fly   red—bed   write—night

When writing a poem, you put your rhyming words at the end of the lines.

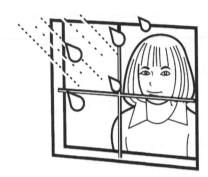

I sit at my secret window and look
At words that swim across my book,
Just like the tiny drops of rain
That swim across my windowpane.

If I could swim into the sky
Like raindrops or a butterfly
Then I would make those swimming words
Into the best poem ever heard.

Think of a topic you would like to write about in a poem. Think of a title for your poem. Write some details to include in your poem. What rhyming words could you use in your poem?

Topic:_____

Title: _____

Some details: _____

_____

_____

Rhyming words: _____

_____

_____

Name _____ Date _____

Writing a Poem, continued

To write a good poem, you should follow these steps.

- Choose a topic for your poem.
- Use colorful words to paint a picture for your audience.
- Use rhyme and rhythm to help express your feelings.
- Use similes to compare things.
- Give your poem a title.

Use your ideas from page 89 to write a poem. Your poem should be at least eight lines long.

Title: _____

_____

_____

_____

_____

_____

_____

_____

_____

_____

_____

_____

_____

90

Writing a Persuasive Paragraph

A **persuasive paragraph** tries to make the reader do something. You may want the reader to accept one side of an issue. An **issue** is an idea that people disagree about. For example, chores can be an issue. Should I do the chores?

Each issue has two sides—pro and con. Pro is for. Con is against. State your side of the issue clearly in a **claim.** A claim is a statement telling which side of the issue you support.

Pro: I should do the chores.
Con: I should not do the chores.

Then you give support. Write three detail sentences supporting your side of the issue. Order your support from weakest point to strongest point.

I should not do the chores because I don't know how.
I am too tired to do the chores.
Doing the chores is not my job.

Read the issue and the claim for the Pro side. Write three support sentences for the Pro side. Then write a Con claim and three support sentences. Use another sheet of paper if necessary.

Issue: Are laws important?

Pro claim: _Laws are important._ _____

Support sentences: _____

_____

_____

Con claim: _____

Support sentences: _____

_____

Writing a Persuasive Paragraph, continued

Remember, your purpose in a persuasive paragraph is to make the reader agree with you. To write a good persuasive paragraph:

- Tell your claim clearly.
- Give your three strongest support points.
- Give your weakest support point first and your strongest point last.
- A good concluding sentence helps a persuasive paragraph. Restate your claim and explain why it is true.

I believe that people should pick up the litter on the streets of our city. I see paper cups and trash everywhere I look. Everyone knows this makes our city look ugly. It has never looked worse than it looks now. Why would anyone want to come here? I think that everyone should stop littering. I also think that everyone should pick up a piece of litter each day. Those are the only ways we can get rid of the litter problem in our city.

Choose one side of the issue about laws on page 91. Use your claim and your support points to write a persuasive paragraph about laws. Be sure your claim is clear. Order your support points from weakest to strongest. Talk directly to your reader. Use another sheet of paper if necessary.

_____

_____

_____

_____

_____

_____

_____

_____

Writing a How-to Paragraph

A **how-to paragraph** is a kind of narrative. It tells how to do a sequence of events, such as tie a shoe or build a birdhouse. You must plan a how-to paragraph carefully.

- Think of all the materials that will be needed.
- Think of all the steps needed to complete the process.
- Be sure your reader knows exactly what to do and when to do it.
- Use time-order words to make the sequence clear.

It is easy to make a seed mosaic. Just glue the seeds onto paper in an interesting pattern. First, you will need to collect seeds of different sizes, shapes, and colors. Then, draw a design on paper. Next, fill in sections of your drawing with glue and seeds. Don't move your paper until the glue dries.

Think of a project you want to tell your reader how to do. Then, think of the materials needed to do the project. Write a list. Finally, write a rough draft of the steps needed to do your project.

Project: _____

Materials needed: _____

_____

_____

Steps to follow:

1. _____

2. _____

3. _____

4. _____

Time-order words you can use: _____

Writing a How-to Paragraph, continued

Writing a how-to paragraph requires careful planning. To write a good how-to paragraph, you should do these things.

- Write a topic sentence that names the project.
- Write a detail sentence that tells what materials are needed.
- Write detail sentences that clearly explain the steps in the process.
- Use time-order words to show the order of the steps. Use words such as *first, next, then,* and *finally.*

Be sure to tell your reader everything that is needed to complete the project.

Use your ideas from page 93 and the tips above to write a how-to paragraph. Use another sheet of paper if necessary.

_____

_____

_____

_____

_____

_____

_____

_____

_____

_____

_____

_____

_____

_____

_____

_____

Writing an Information Paragraph

An **information paragraph** tells facts about one topic. You know the difference between facts and opinions. **Facts** can be proved. **Opinions** are just somebody's ideas. Opinions usually can't be proved.

Fact: Mars is a smaller planet than Earth.

Opinion: I think that creatures from Mars are living among us.

When you write an information paragraph, include only facts. Do not include opinions.

Write *fact* or *opinion* to identify each statement. Then tell why you think it is a fact or an opinion. Should it be included in an information paragraph? Write *yes* or *no*.

_____ **1.** Mars is the fourth planet from the sun.

_____

Include? _____

_____ **2.** Sometimes Mars is only 36 million miles from Earth.

_____

Include? _____

_____ **3.** Mars is a strange planet.

_____

Include? _____

_____ **4.** I think I would rather visit Mars than Venus.

_____

Include? _____

Writing an Information Paragraph, continued

To write an information paragraph, choose one topic. What will you write about that topic? You need a main idea. Suppose you are going to write about eagles. Eagles is your topic. What will your main idea be? What is your focus? You can write many things about eagles. In an information paragraph, you need to develop one main idea about eagles. Your main idea will be your focus. Then you will give details about your main idea.

Topic: eagles
Main idea: Bald eagles are not really bald.
Details: They have white feathers on their head.
                 Long ago the word *bald* meant "white."
                 The eagle was called bald because of its white head feathers.

Choose one of the topics in the box. Then complete the graphic organizer. What can you write about the topic? What will your main idea be? What facts do you know about the topic?

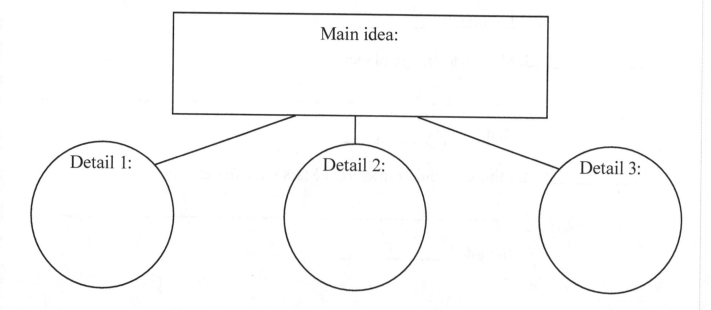

deserts   water   thunder   weasels

Topic: _____

Main idea:

Detail 1:   Detail 2:   Detail 3:

96

Writing an Information Paragraph, continued

To write a good information paragraph:

- Choose one topic to write about.
- Write a topic sentence that tells your main idea about the topic.
- Write at least three detail sentences that tell facts about the main idea.
- Your details should tell who, what, when, where, how, or why.
- Be sure your facts are correct.
- Think of a title for your information paragraph.

You usually have to read about your topic to gather facts. When you read, think about the facts you are learning. Notice how the author organizes these facts and uses them to support main ideas. Then write those facts in your own words. Do not copy them from the place you are reading them. Use your own words. You should also tell about your **source,** or where you read the facts.

Use your graphic organizer from page 96 to write an information paragraph about your topic. If you read about your topic somewhere, write the name of your source. Use another sheet of paper if necessary.

Title: _____

Source: _____

_____

_____

_____

_____

_____

_____

_____

_____

_____

Writing a Response to Literature

A **response to literature** tells an opinion about part of a story. You might tell about a character, a setting, or an event. You should give examples from the story to support your opinion.

An Amazing Animal Journey ——— title of report

The book <u>The Incredible Journey</u> by Sheila Burnford ⎤— title of book (underlined) and author

tells an adventure shared by three pets. A cat named Tao and two dogs named Bodger and Luath work ——— opinion about the events in the book

together and use their smarts to survive against great odds. They travel 300 miles through the Canadian wilderness to find their owners. Along the way, they are chased by wild animals and challenged by nature. They hunt for food and share what they eat. The story ⎦ details from the story that support the opinion

of these animals makes for a great read! Anyone who reads it will love and admire these amazing animals. ⎦ a conclusion sentence that sums up the response

Think of a book you would like to tell about. Then use the writing plan below to organize your report. Use another sheet of paper if necessary.

The title and author: _____

A one-sentence opinion of the book:

_____

_____

My opinion about the characters, events, or setting:

_____

_____

Details that support my opinion:

_____

_____

_____

Name _____   Date _____

Writing a Response to Literature, continued

To write a good response to literature, you should follow these steps.

- Choose one book to write about.
- Write a title. Try to use words from the response in the title.
- Name the book and author in your response. Underline the book title.

- Decide if you want to write mostly about the events, the characters, or the setting.
- Give your opinion of the events, characters, or setting. Tell your reasons for your opinion.
- Include details that support your ideas.
- End with a conclusion that sums up the response.

Use your writing plan on page 98 to write a response to literature. Use another sheet of paper if necessary.

Title: _____

_____

_____

_____

_____

_____

_____

_____

_____

_____

_____

Writing an Opinion Paragraph

We don't all have the same opinions. In fact, sometimes we have very different beliefs or ideas. You can write about your beliefs in an **opinion paragraph**. When you write an opinion paragraph, always include reasons. **Reasons** tell why you believe what you do. Remember that you cannot prove an opinion is true. But you can give reasons for your opinion!

Opinion: Recess is an important part of the day.

Reason: During recess, students learn how to play well with others.

Write *yes* or *no* to tell whether each reason supports the opinion.

1. **Opinion:** Fried foods should not be on the school lunch menu.

   _____ **a.** Fried foods are unhealthy.

   _____ **b.** Students should eat vegetables and fruits, not fried foods.

   _____ **c.** Fried foods taste good.

   _____ **d.** Fried foods cause weight gain.

2. **Opinion:** The telephone is the most important invention.

   _____ **a.** The telephone helps us communicate.

   _____ **b.** The telephone does not need a lot of repair work.

   _____ **c.** The telephone helps us learn when we use it to find information.

   _____ **d.** The telephone comes in different sizes.

Writing an Opinion Paragraph, continued

> Choose a topic. Then, decide what you believe about that topic. For example, you might write about holidays. Perhaps you think that Memorial Day is the best holiday. Your opinion will be your topic sentence. Then you need to decide which two or three reasons you can use to support your topic sentence.
>
> Topic: holidays
>
> Opinion (Topic Sentence): Memorial Day is the best holiday.
>
> Reason 1: Memorial Day honors people who died in wars.
>
> Reason 2: My family has a picnic on Memorial Day.
>
> Reason 3: Memorial Day marks the beginning of summer.

Choose a topic for your paragraph. Decide your opinion about the topic. Your opinion is your main idea. Then write two or three reasons why you believe this opinion. Tell your most important reason first.

Topic: _____

Main Idea (Opinion)

Reason 1: _____

_____

Reason 2: _____

_____

Reason 3: _____

_____

Name _____ Date _____

Writing an Opinion Paragraph, continued

You've come up with reasons for your opinion. Now think of facts and details that support each reason. Notice how the writer of this opinion paragraph has facts and details that support the reasons. The writer tells the most important reason first. The last sentence sums up the writer's opinion.

Memorial Day

In my opinion, Memorial Day is the best holiday of the year. **One reason** is that Memorial Day is a day when we say thank-you to our troops. We honor the men and women who have died at war. **Another reason** is that Memorial Day is a chance for families to have fun. **For example,** some families have picnics. **Finally,** Memorial Day marks the beginning of summer. It is the day our local pool opens. Memorial Day is a way to honor important people and also have a great time!

Write your reasons from page 101. Then write a fact or detail that supports each reason.

Reason 1: _____

Fact or detail that supports the reason: _____

Reason 2: _____

Fact or detail that supports the reason: _____

Reason 3: _____

Fact or detail that supports the reason: _____

© Houghton Mifflin Harcourt Publishing Company

Unit 4
Core Skills Writing, Grade 4

Writing an Opinion Paragraph, continued

To write a good opinion paragraph, follow these steps.

- Write your topic and your opinion from page 101. This is your first sentence.
- Next, write each reason and then support it with facts or details.
- Link your ideas with transitions. See the box for some ideas.
- In the final sentence, tell why your opinion makes sense.

Transitions
because
for example
in addition
for instance
finally

Write your opinion paragraph. Use another sheet of paper if necessary.

Title: _____

_____

_____

_____

_____

_____

_____

_____

_____

_____

_____

_____

_____

_____

_____

Name _____ Date _____

Writing an Informative Report

Are you ready for a challenge? Do you think you can write a report? Keep in mind that your report must be five paragraphs long. You need an introduction paragraph, three body paragraphs that give details, and a conclusion paragraph. Who can write that much? Well, let's give it a try.

First, you need to choose a topic and a focus. Suppose you are assigned to write a short report on oceans. What would you do? You can begin the process by asking yourself some questions. Remember, this is the brainstorming or prewriting part.

What am I supposed to write about? _____

Can I write all about the oceans in 500 words? No, I have to narrow my topic.

What do I know about the oceans? _____

_____

OK, now you have done a little brainstorming. Most work on an informative report is done before the writing begins. There are many things about the oceans you could write about. Let's try narrowing some topics.

oceans ⟶ names and locations ⟶ comparison of sizes

oceans ⟶ ocean life ⟶ coral reef habitat

Now you try it. Think of another ocean topic and narrow the topic on the lines below.

oceans ⟶ _____ ⟶ _____

Let's say you are going to write a short report on coral reefs as habitats. The first thing you need is a thesis statement. A thesis statement tells what you will write about in the report. The thesis statement usually goes at the end of the introduction paragraph.

Thesis statement #1: Coral reefs are an important habitat for ocean life.

Now write a thesis statement for the topic you narrowed above.

Thesis statement #2: _____

_____

Name _____   Date _____

Taking Notes

Let's say you are reading a **source** about your topic. A source is where you get information. It can be a book, a magazine, or the Internet. There are many sources to consider for your report. (As you are reading, look for pictures you can include, too.)

As you read, look for words you can use in your report. You will find important vocabulary words related to your topic. Make sure you understand what they mean. Using precise words will show you know your topic well!

You find some information you want to use in your report. You decide to take notes. Two ways to take notes are **paraphrases** and **direct quotes.**

- You use a **paraphrase** to restate some information in your own words. A good paraphrase shows you are thinking about your topic. You are reading carefully.
- To paraphrase, you must first read the source carefully. Then close the source. Think about what you have read. Write the ideas using your own words.
- Copying words from a source and changing a few of them is bad paraphrasing. You must write the information in your own words.
- Always remember to write the title of the source, the author, and the pages where you found the information.

Carefully read the information in the sentence below. Next put a sheet of paper over the sentence. Count to 50. On your own paper, write the information in your own words. Write the information two different ways.

Coral reefs provide an inviting habitat for many kinds of sea creatures.

Direct Quotes

Sometimes the information you find is very important. You can't write the information better in your own words. In this case, you can write a **direct quote.**

- A direct quote uses words as they appear in the source. You copy the words exactly from the source. You put **quotation marks** at each end of the direct quote.

    "Coral reefs provide an inviting habitat" for many different types of sea life.

- If the direct quote includes the end of a sentence, the period goes inside the quotation marks.

    Coral reefs serve as a "habitat for many kinds of sea creatures."

Do not use many direct quotes in your report. If you do, then you are not doing much writing, are you? You are just copying someone else's writing.

Read the paragraph carefully. Answer each question by writing a direct quote from the paragraph. Remember to enclose the direct quote in quotation marks.

Coral reefs are usually located in clear, warm oceans. Coral reefs need sunlight to live, so they are often at the surface of the ocean. Coral reefs are home to about one fourth of all sea life. Some creatures that live in a coral reef are sponges, worms, fish, sharks, and shrimp.

1. Where are coral reefs usually found? _____

_____

2. Why are coral reefs often at the surface of the ocean? _____

_____

3. About how many of the ocean's creatures live in coral reefs? _____

_____

A Writing Plan: Outlining

You have been using writing plans for your paragraphs. You need a writing plan for your report, too. A longer writing plan is called an **outline.** An outline lists the main ideas of a topic.

- Start your outline with a **thesis statement** that tells the focus of the writing.
- Next write your main headings and subheadings. These parts tell what goes in each body paragraph of your report.
- Main headings start with a Roman numeral. Subheadings start with a capital letter.
- Each Roman numeral should represent a paragraph.

Thesis statement: Coral reefs are an important habitat for ocean life.

   I. Coral animals
      A. Tiny sea creatures
      B. Live in colonies
      C. Skeletons of dead coral form reef

  II. Location of coral reefs
      A. Warm salt water
      B. Often near surface of water
      C. Can be very large

 III. Animals that live in coral reefs
      A. Fish
      B. Shrimp and lobsters
      C. Worms

Answer the questions.

1. What would be the topics of the three body paragraphs?

_____

_____

2. What would be a detail from the third body paragraph?

_____

_____

A Writing Plan: Outlining, continued

Read the paragraph below. Then outline the contents of the paragraph. Remember to use a Roman numeral for the main heading and capital letters for the subheadings.

Coral animals live together in a colony, or group. They attach themselves to each other by thin tissue. A coral colony can be very big. As coral animals reproduce, the older ones die. Their skeletons stay where they are. New coral animals attach themselves to the skeletons. As time passes, the colonies grow. Colonies can grow in different shapes. Some look like heads of cabbage. Others look like trees without leaves.

_____

_____

_____

_____

_____

_____

_____

_____

_____

_____

_____

_____

_____

_____

_____

Beginning and Ending a Report

An **introduction paragraph** introduces your report. It gives your reader some general information about your topic.

- Write a catchy beginning sentence. Try to grab your reader's interest.
- Name your topic in your introduction.
- Tell some general details about your topic.
- Write a **thesis statement** for your report. A thesis statement is like a topic sentence. It gives the focus of your report. It tells how you have narrowed your topic.

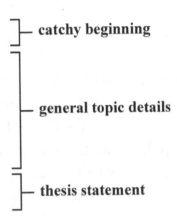

Do you think a coral is a place to keep horses? Well, it's not. A coral is a tiny sea creature. Corals live together in colonies in warm salt water. The colonies grow and form coral reefs. Some coral reefs are huge. They can be hundreds of miles long. Many sea creatures live in the coral reefs. **Coral reefs are an important habitat for ocean life.**

— catchy beginning

— general topic details

— thesis statement

A **conclusion paragraph** ends your report. You don't just want to stop writing after your last body paragraph. You want to let your reader know what he or she has just read in your report.

- Restate your thesis statement in different words.
- Summarize details from your report.
- Tell the reader why the topic is important.

Read the sample introduction paragraph in the box above. Use the introduction paragraph and what you know about coral reefs to write a conclusion paragraph. Remember to restate the thesis statement in your own words. Summarize details about coral reefs as important habitats. Use another sheet of paper.

Writing Your Report

Writing an informative report takes a lot of time and hard work. You will do better if you have a plan. Try following the steps below.

Step 1: Choose a topic. Think about your audience and your purpose. Choose a writing pattern.

Step 2: Narrow your topic. Write a thesis statement.

Step 3: Find some sources. Begin by looking up your topic in an encyclopedia. You can also search on the Internet.

Step 4: Take notes. Remember, you can summarize or paraphrase information. You can also write direct quotes.

Step 5: Build a writing plan. An outline is a good writing plan. Each Roman numeral should be a paragraph in your report.

Step 6: Write an introduction paragraph. Your introduction should have a catchy beginning. It should name your topic and include general details. It should also contain your thesis statement.

Step 7: Write a rough draft of your body paragraphs. Remember to use your writing plan. Link your ideas using transition words and phrases. Here are some ideas and phrases you can use to connect ideas: *for example, however, because, also, as a result, first, after, then, in the end,* and *according to.*

Step 8: Write a conclusion paragraph. Remember to restate your thesis in different words. You should also summarize details from your report.

Step 9: Put your report aside for a day or two. Then read it again. What kind of revisions can you make? How can your report be improved? Write another draft.

Step 10: Proofread and edit your second draft. Make corrections.

Step 11: Write your final draft. Be sure to proofread your final draft, too.

Step 12: Publish your report. Include a cover sheet with a title and drawings or pictures if possible.

Use the 12 steps above to write an informative report. Write your report on another sheet of paper or type it on a computer.

Prewriting Survey

My Purpose

1. What am I writing about?

   _____

2. What do I want to say?

   _____

   _____

3. What is my purpose for writing? Explain.

   _____

   _____

My Audience

4. Who will be reading my writing? What do I know about the people who will read what I write?

   _____

   _____

5. What does my audience already know about my topic? What new information will I tell my audience?

   _____

   _____

6. How will I share my writing with my audience?

   _____

   _____

Prewriting Survey, continued

Writing Purpose and Details

7. Why am I writing? Choose one purpose below and write the details you want to share.

To inform (to give facts about a topic)	Who What Where	When Why How
To express (to share a feeling or idea)	What I see What I hear What I touch What I smell What I taste	
To entertain (to make the reader experience an emotion)	Feelings Strong words Stories Memories	
To persuade (to make the reader think or act a certain way)	My opinion Facts that support my opinion	

Writing Pattern

8. Which writing pattern will I use to achieve my purpose?

Main idea and details   Sequence of events   Compare and contrast

Problem and solution   Cause and effect   Summary

Planning

9. Which graphic organizer can help me plan the details of my writing? Circle all that you could use.

Main idea and details web   Sequence chart   Cause and effect chart

Problem and solution chart   Venn diagram   Summary chart

Name _____ Date _____

Writing Traits Checklist

Title _____

Trait	Strong	Average	Needs Improvement
Ideas			
The main idea of my writing is interesting.			
The topic is just the right size. I have good focus.			
The main idea is written clearly in one sentence.			
I have strong supporting details about the main idea.			
Organization			
The form of writing makes the information clear.			
My writing has a beginning, a middle, and an end.			
The details are in the right order.			
I use transition words to connect my ideas.			
My first sentence catches the reader's interest.			
My last sentence restates the main idea.			
Voice			
I show what I think or feel about the topic.			
I use the right tone for my writing: funny, serious, sad.			
I use words that my audience will understand.			
Word Choice			
I use the five senses to describe things.			
I use strong action words to tell what is happening.			
I use specific words in my writing.			
I use new words in my writing when needed.			

Name _____ Date _____

Writing Traits Checklist, continued

Trait	Strong	Average	Needs Improvement
Sentence Fluency			
I have sentences that are short, medium, and long.			
I avoid repeating the same sentence pattern again and again.			
I use the same verb tense throughout the writing.			
I write sentences that begin with different parts of speech.			
Conventions			
All sentences begin with a capital letter.			
All sentences end with the correct punctuation.			
All subjects and verbs agree with each other.			
All pronouns and nouns agree with each other.			
I use an apostrophe to show possession.			
I use a comma to join two sentences with *and, or,* or *but.*			
I use a comma to separate items in a series.			
I use quotation marks to write dialogue or a quote.			
I indent the first line of each paragraph.			
Presentation			
My writing has a title.			
I use pictures, charts, or diagrams to support the ideas in my writing.			
The final copy is clean and neat.			
My drawing or writing is neat and easy to read.			
I have a cover and title page.			

Proofreading Checklist

You should proofread your work before you publish it. When you proofread, you look at your writing for mistakes. Proofread your work several times to search for mistakes. This list will help you proofread. You can also use it to proofread a classmate's writing.

Capitalization

- ☐ Do all sentences begin with a capital letter?
- ☐ Are titles, people's names, and names of particular places capitalized?
- ☐ Are the months and days of the week capitalized?

Punctuation

- ☐ Is there a period at the end of each abbreviation?
- ☐ Does a comma separate items in a series?
- ☐ Does a comma correctly separate a quotation from the rest of a sentence?
- ☐ Are quotation marks used around the words that people say in dialogue?
- ☐ Are quotation marks used around a direct quote from a source?
- ☐ Are apostrophes used to show possession?

Spelling

- ☐ Are all the words spelled correctly?
- ☐ Did I use a dictionary to check words that might be misspelled?

Grammar and Usage

- ☐ Do subjects and verbs agree in number?
- ☐ Do nouns and pronouns agree in number?
- ☐ Are there any sentence fragments or run-on sentences?
- ☐ Are there any double negatives?

Proofreading Marks

Use the marks below to edit your writing.

≡ Use a capital letter.

⊙ Add a period.

∧ Add something.

⋏ Add a comma.

ⱽ ⱽ Add quotation marks.

ℰ Cut something.

⋀ Replace something.

⋔ Transpose.

◯ Spell correctly.

⌗ Indent paragraph.

∕ Make a lowercase letter.

116

Publishing Your Writing

There are many ways you can use technology to write. You can use e-mail to send your writing to someone. Be sure you have the address of the person you want to send it to. Use a subject line that tells what your e-mail is about. Be specific to get your reader's attention. Write a formal e-mail in a letter format, with a greeting and a closing.

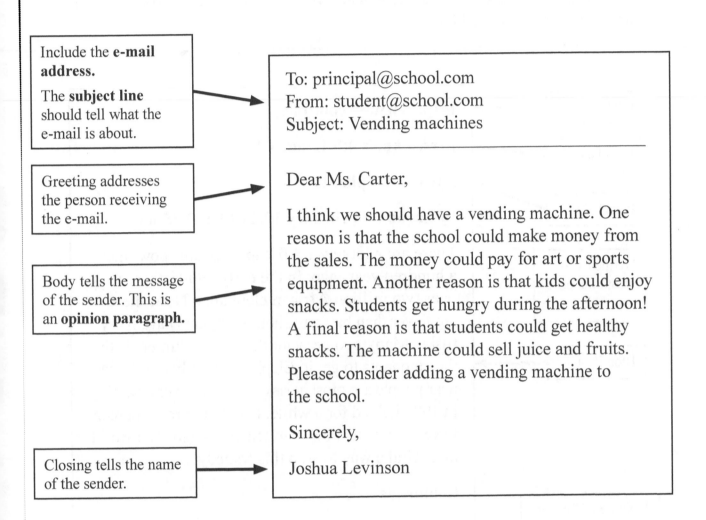

Include the **e-mail address.**

The **subject line** should tell what the e-mail is about.

Greeting addresses the person receiving the e-mail.

Body tells the message of the sender. This is an **opinion paragraph.**

Closing tells the name of the sender.

To: principal@school.com
From: student@school.com
Subject: Vending machines

Dear Ms. Carter,

I think we should have a vending machine. One reason is that the school could make money from the sales. The money could pay for art or sports equipment. Another reason is that kids could enjoy snacks. Students get hungry during the afternoon! A final reason is that students could get healthy snacks. The machine could sell juice and fruits. Please consider adding a vending machine to the school.

Sincerely,

Joshua Levinson

Publishing Your Writing, continued

Blog Post

The word **blog** is short for "weblog." A blog is a journal that you keep on the Internet so that other people can read and comment. You can use a blog to share news about yourself with others. Blogs can also be essays or include opinions. You can publish your writing for class on your class blog. Ask your teacher to show you how to publish to your class blog. Notice the important parts of a blog.

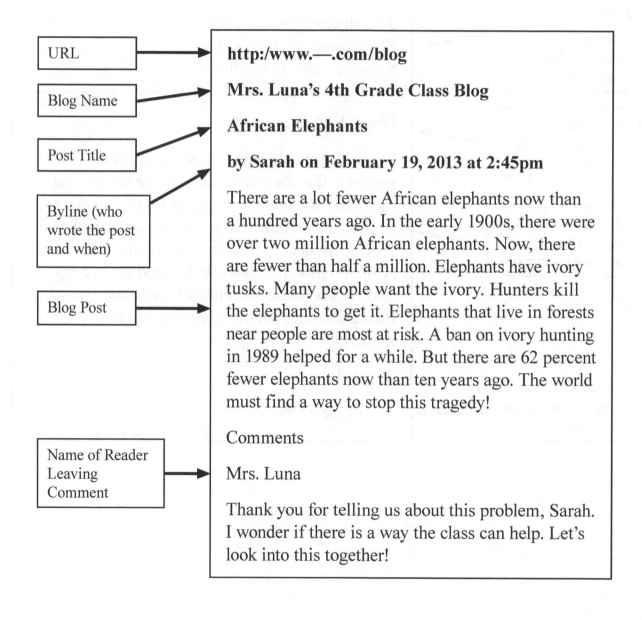

URL	http://www.—.com/blog
Blog Name	**Mrs. Luna's 4th Grade Class Blog**
Post Title	**African Elephants**
Byline (who wrote the post and when)	**by Sarah on February 19, 2013 at 2:45pm**
Blog Post	There are a lot fewer African elephants now than a hundred years ago. In the early 1900s, there were over two million African elephants. Now, there are fewer than half a million. Elephants have ivory tusks. Many people want the ivory. Hunters kill the elephants to get it. Elephants that live in forests near people are most at risk. A ban on ivory hunting in 1989 helped for a while. But there are 62 percent fewer elephants now than ten years ago. The world must find a way to stop this tragedy!
	Comments
Name of Reader Leaving Comment	Mrs. Luna
	Thank you for telling us about this problem, Sarah. I wonder if there is a way the class can help. Let's look into this together!

Self-Evaluation Checklist

Title _____

	Yes	No

1. Did I take time to prewrite and brainstorm about my topic? _____ _____

2. Did I think about my audience? _____ _____

3. Did I choose the right purpose and form for my topic? _____ _____

4. Do I have good focus about my topic? _____ _____

5. Is my writing clear and easy to understand? _____ _____

6. Is the main idea of each sentence clear and direct? _____ _____

7. Did I present information in a logical order? _____ _____

8. Did I choose interesting and specific words? _____ _____

9. Are my verbs and adjectives lively and interesting? _____ _____

10. Did I add details, examples, facts, explanations, or direct quotes to strengthen my writing? _____ _____

11. Did I remove unnecessary information? _____ _____

12. Did I follow basic rules for capitalization, punctuation, spelling, grammar, and usage? _____ _____

13. Did I link events and ideas with transition words? _____ _____

14. Do my sentences have good rhythm and flow? _____ _____

15. Did I revise confusing parts to make them clearer? _____ _____

16. Did I choose a title that grabs my reader's attention? _____ _____

17. Is my writing neat and easy to read? _____ _____

18. Have I done my best work on this piece of writing? _____ _____

Sentence Graphic Organizers

Use these graphic organizers to diagram sentences. You can add lines under the main idea line if needed.

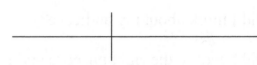

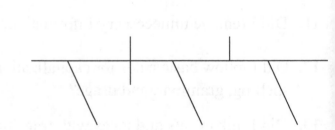

Main Idea and Details Web

Write the main idea in the oval. Write five strong details in the circles. Think about specific and lively words that you could use in your writing to tell about the details. Write these words in the rectangles.

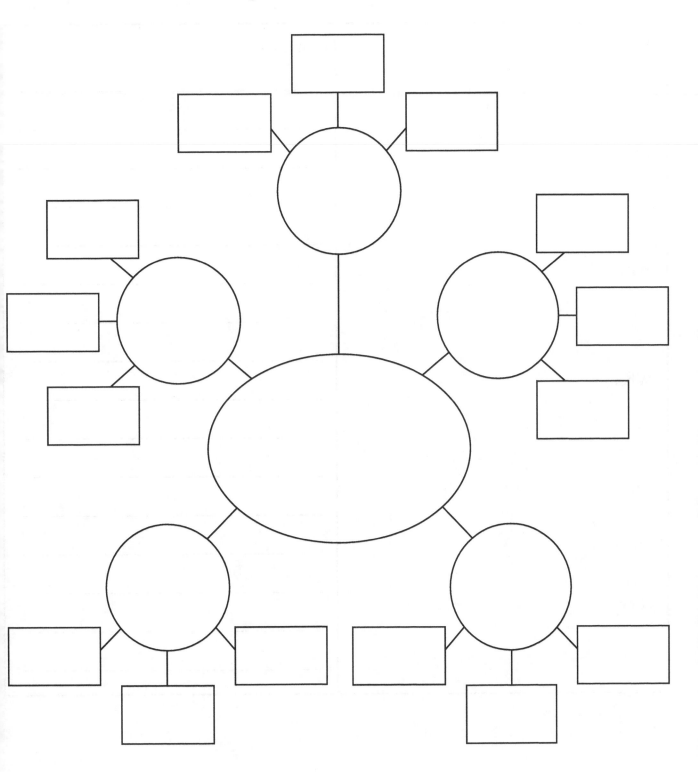

Summary Chart

Write the details on the left side of the chart. Write a summary on the right side of the chart. Try to include all the information in as few sentences as you can.

Who	Summary
	_____
	_____
What	_____
	_____
Where	_____
	_____
When	_____
	_____
Why	_____
	_____
How	_____
	_____

Problem and Solution Chart

Name the problem in the first box. Then write details about the problem. Name the solution that would fix the problem. Give details to explain why the solution would work.

Problem	Details About Problem (Why is it a problem?)

Solution	Details About Solution (Why is it a good solution?)

Cause and Effect Chart

Write what happened in the Effect box. Write the reason it happened in the Cause box.

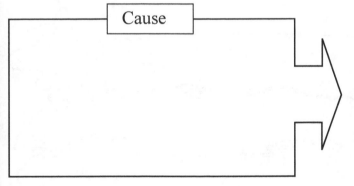

Cause

Effect

Paragraph Structure Chart

Use the graphic organizer to plan your paragraph. Write your topic sentence and concluding sentence on the pieces of bread. Write your details between the slices.

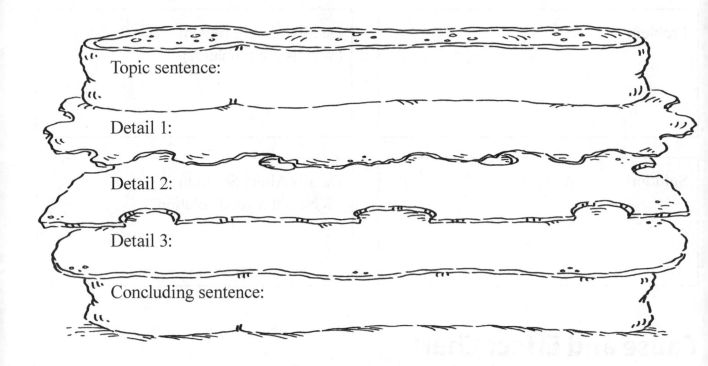

Topic sentence:

Detail 1:

Detail 2:

Detail 3:

Concluding sentence:

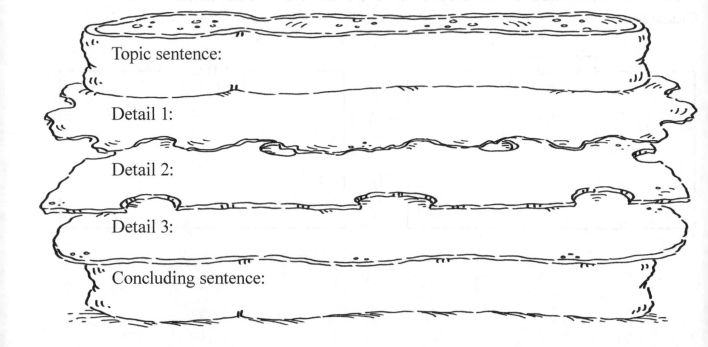

Topic sentence:

Detail 1:

Detail 2:

Detail 3:

Concluding sentence:

Glossary

action verb (page 6) a verb that shows action

active verb (page 47) a verb that shows action done by the subject of the sentence

adjective (pages 7, 24) a word that modifies a noun or pronoun

adverb (pages 7, 26) a word that modifies a verb, an adjective, or another adverb

audience (page 2) the ones who will read what you write

blog (page 118) a journal that is kept on the Internet so people can read and comment

brainstorming (page 9) to think about ideas for your writing

cause (page 73) why something has happened

character (page 83) real or made-up people or animals in a narrative

claim (page 91) a statement about which side of the issue you support

clause (page 29) a group of related words that includes a subject and a predicate

comma (page 42) a mark of punctuation used to separate the parts of a compound sentence or a series

common noun (page 5) a word that names any person, place, or thing; begins with a lowercase letter

compare (page 71) to show how two things are alike

complete predicate (page 16) the simple predicate and all the words that describe it

complete subject (page 16) the simple subject and all the words that describe it

compound predicate (page 35) a predicate containing two or more simple predicates

compound sentence (page 41) a sentence that is made up of two or more simple sentences

compound subject (page 34) a subject containing two or more simple subjects

concluding sentence (page 61) restates the main idea and summarizes the information in the paragraph

conclusion paragraph (page 109) the last paragraph in a report or long piece of writing

conjunction (page 8, 33) a word that connects words or groups of words

connective (page 8) a word that joins parts of a sentence

contrast (page 71) to show how two things are different

conventions (page 13) the rules of grammar and writing

declarative sentence (page 38) a sentence that makes a statement

describe (page 80) to tell what something is like; to paint a picture with words

details (page 23) words that tell whose, which, when, where, and how about the main idea

detail sentences (page 61) body sentences that tell more about the main idea of a paragraph

dialogue (page 85) words said by characters in a narrative

direct object (page 19) receiver of the action in a sentence

direct quote (page 105) exact words from a source

double negative (page 27) two negatives used incorrectly in a sentence

draft (page 15) a version of a piece of writing

edit (page 15) to correct errors you have made in writing

effect (page 73) something that has been caused to happen

entertain (page 3) to please or amuse the reader

exclamation mark (page 40) a mark of punctuation used at the end of an exclamatory or imperative sentence

exclamatory sentence (page 39) a sentence that shows excitement or strong feeling

express (page 3) to tell your personal feelings

fact (page 95) a statement that can be proved

figurative language (page 52) words used to compare unlike things

focus (page 63) to narrow a topic

future tense verb (page 48) a verb that tells what will happen in the future

helping verb (page 20) a verb that comes before the main verb in a sentence

how-to paragraph (page 93) tells how to do a sequence of events

ideas (page 11) what you have to say or write about a topic

imperative sentence (page 39) a sentence that makes a request or gives a command

indent (page 62) move in five spaces from the left margin

independent clause (page 29) a clause that is a complete sentence and shows a complete thought

inform (page 3) to tell facts about a topic

information paragraph (page 95) tells facts about one topic

interrogative sentence (page 38) a sentence that asks a question

introduction paragraph (page 109) the first paragraph in a report or long piece of writing

issue (page 91) an idea that people disagree about

journal (page 4) a record of daily events

linking verb (page 21) a verb that links the subject to a noun or an adjective in the complete predicate

main idea (page 17) what a piece of writing is mainly about

modifier (page 7) a word or group of words that changes the meaning of another word

narrate (page 83) tell about a sequence of events

narrative (page 83) a factual or fictional story

negative (page 27) a word that means "no" or "not"

noun (page 5) a word that names a person, place, or thing

object of the preposition (page 30) the noun or pronoun that follows a preposition

object pronoun (page 5) used as the object of a sentence

opinion (page 95) someone's belief that cannot be proved

opinion paragraph (page 100) tells a belief about a topic with reasons supported by facts and details

organization (page 11) the way you arrange the ideas you are writing

outcome (page 83) the ending of a narrative

outline (page 107) a writing plan for the content of a report

paragraph (page 61) a group of sentences that tells about one main idea

paraphrase (page 105) to restate someone else's ideas in your own words

passive verb (page 47) a verb that shows being and not action

past tense verb (page 48) a verb that tells what happened in the past

period (page 40) a mark of punctuation used at the end of a declarative sentence or an abbreviation

personal narrative (page 84) a story about something you have done

persuade (page 3) to try to convince the reader to do something

persuasive paragraph (page 91) tries to make the reader do something

phrase (page 29) a group of words that does not have a subject or a predicate

plural verb (page 18) a verb that agrees with a plural subject

predicate (page 16) the part of a sentence that tells what the subject is or does

preposition (page 8) a word that shows the relation of a noun or pronoun to another word in a sentence

prepositional phrase (page 30) a phrase made up of a preposition, its object, and any other words

present tense verb (page 6) a verb that tells what is happening now

presentation (page 13) the way words and pictures look on the page

prewriting (page 9) to think about what and why you are writing

problem (page 72) something that is wrong

pronoun (page 5) a word that takes the place of a noun

proofread (page 10) to search for errors you have made in writing

proper noun (page 5) a word that names a particular person, place, or thing; begins with a capital letter

publish (page 10) to share your writing with others (sometimes using technology)

purpose (page 3) your reason for writing

question mark (page 40) a mark of punctuation used at the end of an interrogative sentence

quotation marks (page 106) punctuation marks that are placed at each end of a direct quote

response to literature (page 98) tells the writer's opinion about events, a setting, or a character from a story and includes details that support the opinion

revising (page 10) to think more about what you have written to make it better

run-on sentence (page 58) a sentence error caused by incorrect punctuation

sentence (page 16) a group of words that tells a complete thought

sentence fluency (page 13) when sentences have rhythm and flow

sentence fragment (page 57) a part of a sentence that does not tell a complete idea

sequence (page 70) a series of events in order

series (page 45) a list of three or more words or items

setting (page 83) where and when the events of a narrative take place

simile (page 52) compares two things by using *like* or *as*

simple predicate (page 17) the main verb in the complete predicate

simple sentence (page 41) a complete sentence that contains only one complete thought

simple subject (page 17) the main noun or pronoun in the complete subject

singular verb (page 18) a verb that agrees with a singular subject

solution (page 72) the way to fix a problem

source (page 105) where you find information

subject (page 16) who or what a sentence is about

subject pronoun (page 5) used as the subject of a sentence

summarize (page 74) to tell the key details of an event or a piece of writing

synonyms (page 49) words that have the same general meaning

tense (page 6) the time a verb tells

thesis statement (page 109) a sentence that tells the focus of a report or long piece of writing

time-order words (page 66) transition words that show movement in time

topic (page 14) what you are writing about

topic sentence (page 61) tells the main idea of the paragraph

trait (page 11) a skill

transition (page 66) a word that links ideas from one sentence to the next

unity (page 75) when all the parts of a paragraph tell about one main idea

unnecessary information (page 75) information that does not belong in a paragraph

verb (page 6) a word that shows action or connects the subject to another word in a sentence

verb phrase (page 20) the main verb and its helpers in a sentence

verb tense (page 48) the time a verb tells

voice (page 12) the way a writer "speaks" to the reader through writing

word choice (page 12) the words you pick to express your ideas

Answer Key

Student answers will vary on the pages not included in this Answer Key. Accept all reasonable answers.

Page 1

1. C
2. B
3. D
4. A

Page 2

Answers will vary. Possible answers include:

1. the writer, close friends
2. adults, citizens, people at a city meeting
3. friends, family members
4. students, teachers, principal

Page 3

1. D
2. C
3. B
4. A

Page 5

1. shells, sand
2. books, shelf
3. I, me, my
4. we, us, they, them

Page 8

1. addition of two things
2. a choice between two things
3. a difference between two things
4.–5. Answers will vary.

Page 10

Correct order: 2, 4, 1, 5, 3

Pages 11–13

1. traits
2. ideas
3. organization
4. words
5. voice
6. presentation
7. conventions
8. fluency

Pages 14–15

1. imagination
2. interest
3. topic
4. organize
5. outline
6. draft
7. ideas
8. aloud

Page 16

1. yes
2. no
3. no
4. yes
5.–8. Answers will vary.

Page 19

1. corn
2. cans
3. watermelon
4. stars
5. me
6. sentences

Page 26

Answers may vary.

1. slowly
2. yesterday
3. here
4. happily

Page 27

1. ever
2. any
3. anything
4. anybody
5. is

Page 29

1. Clause: Fish swim; Phrase: in the pond
2. Clause: Geese honk; Phrase: in the evening
3. Clause: Jess found the puppy; Phrase: by the lake
4. Clause: The girl sat; Phrase: on the porch
5. Clause: the trains run; Phrase: In the morning

Page 33

1. and
2. or
3. but
4. and
5. but
6. or
7. and
8. or

Page 36

1. is
2. are
3. are
4. are
5.–7. Answers will vary.

Page 44

Answers may vary.

1. The princess entered and disappeared in the mist.
2. The king and the queen could not find the princess.
3. Maybe the blue mist and the princess will return someday.

Page 45

Answers may vary.

1. Jenna, Carlos, and Ashley are studying.
2. People should eat less, walk more, and exercise often.
3. Air pollution is smelly, dirty, and unsafe.
4. The snow was cold, wet, and mushy.

Page 49

Answers may vary.

1. Tales
2. trips
3. courageous
4. big
5. problems

Page 57

Sentence 2 is not a fragment.

Page 58

Answers may vary.
1. He studied hard. He hoped to pass the test.
2. We paddled a canoe, and we swam in the lake.
3. Jana found a lost puppy. It was cold and wet.
4. Kyle searched for the keys, but he could not find them.

Page 59

1. B
2. E
3. A
4. D
5. C

Page 60

Answers may vary.
1. Did you see those flying saucers?
2. I didn't see any flying saucers.
3. The three dogs eat an apple.
4. I found money at the mall, and I gave it to the guard.

Page 61

Students should suggest that the second paragraph is better. The first paragraph does not stay on topic.

Page 62

1. eating spaghetti
2. Eating spaghetti is fun, but it can be a little dangerous.
3. Answers will vary.
4. For me, spaghetti is the perfect meal, even if it is messy.

Page 66

Correct order: 1, 5, 3, 4, 2, 6

Page 68

Answers may vary.
1. sad
2. serious
3. funny

Page 75

Reasons will vary but should suggest the unnecessary information is not about the topic.
1. Unnecessary information: Kangaroos live in Australia, too.
2. Unnecessary information: She went to the store and bought some pickles for her sandwich.

Page 77

Errors include spelling, capitalization, subject-verb disagreement, and punctuation. The correct paragraph follows:

Windmills are machines that use wind power. They are used to provide power to pump water or to generate electricity. Most windmills have a wheel of blades that is turned by the wind. The shaft of the wheel is mounted on a tower. The shaft is connected to a system of gears. These gears carry power to a water pump or an electric generator.

Page 87

Answers will vary.
1. The boy bought a bag of apples at the supermarket.
2. The playroom was filled with toys.
3. The two girls and three boys observed giraffes, monkeys, and tigers at the zoo.
4. The clown handed the woman a rose.

Page 88

Answers may vary.
a sight: 25 red balloons in the classroom
a smell: freshly cut grass
a feeling: cool breeze
a sound: children laughing

Page 95

Reasons will vary.
1. fact; include
2. fact; include
3. opinion; do not include
4. opinion; do not include

Page 100

Answers will vary.
1. a. Yes
   b. Yes
   c. No
   d. Yes
2. a. Yes
   b. No
   c. Yes
   d. No

Page 106

Answers may vary.
1. "Coral reefs are usually located in clear, warm oceans."
2. "Coral reefs need sunlight to live, so they are often at the surface of the ocean."
3. "Coral reefs are home to about one fourth of all sea life."

Page 107

1. Coral animals, location of coral reefs, animals that live in coral reefs
2. Answers will vary. Possible answers are: fish, shrimp and lobsters, or worms.

Page 108

Outlines may vary.
I. Corals live in colonies.
   A. Corals attach to each other.
   B. Colonies can be large.
   C. Skeletons become part of colony.
   D. Colonies have different shapes.

Answer Key
Core Skills Writing, Grade 4

4500799069-0607-2020

Printed in the U.S.A